WILLIAMS-SONOMA
PASTA COLLECTION

RISOTTO

WILLIAMS-SONOMA
PASTA COLLECTION

RISOTTO

GENERAL EDITOR
CHUCK WILLIAMS

RECIPES BY
KRISTINE KIDD

PHOTOGRAPHY BY
JOYCE OUDKERK POOL

WELDON OWEN

WILLIAMS-SONOMA
Founder: Chuck Williams

WELDON OWEN INC.
President: John Owen
Vice President and Publisher: Wendely Harvey
Managing Editor: Jill Fox
Recipe Analysis: Hill Nutrition Associates Inc.
    Lynne S. Hill, MS, RD; William A. Hill, MS, RD
Copy Editor: Carolyn Miller
Art Director: John Bull
Designer: Patty Hill
Production Director: Stephanie Sherman
Production Editor: Janique Gascoigne
Editorial Assistants: Stephani Grant, Marguerite Ozburn
Co-Editions Director: Derek Barton
Co-Editions Production Manager: Tarji Mickelson
Food Stylist: Susan Massey
Food Stylist Assistants: Andrea Lucich, Geri Lesko
Prop Stylist: Carol Hacker
Photographer's Assistant: Myriam Varela
Hand Model: Tracey Hughes
Indexer: ALTA Indexing Service
Proofreaders: Desne Border, Ken DellaPenta
Illustrator: Nicole Kaufman
Props Courtesy: Biordi, Pottery Barn, Williams-Sonoma
Special Thanks: James Badham, Mick Bagnato, Peggy Fallon,
    William Garry, Santiago Homsi Jr., Bryan's Meats, Cal-Mart

A Weldon Owen Production

First printed in 1996
10 9 8 7 6 5 4 3 2 1

Library of Congress
Cataloging-in-Publication Data:

Kidd, Kristine.
    Risotto / general editor, Chuck Williams ;
    recipes by Kristine Kidd ; photography by Joyce Oudkerk Pool
    p.   cm. — (Williams-Sonoma pasta collection)
    Includes index.
    ISBN 1-875137-08-4
    1.   Cookery (Rice)
    I. Williams, Chuck.   II. Title.   III. Series.
    TX809.R5K53 1996
    641.6'318—dc20   95-24285
                        CIP

All recipes include customary U.S. and metric measurements. Metric
conversions are based on a standard developed for this book and have
been rounded off. Actual weights may vary. Unless otherwise stated,
the recipes were designed for medium-sized fruits and vegetables.

*Cover: Risotto with Red Bell Pepper, Tomato, Mint and Feta (recipe on page 18)
features traditional Mediterranean flavors in a colorful mix.*

The Williams-Sonoma Pasta Collection
conceived and produced by Weldon Owen Inc.
814 Montgomery Street, San Francisco, CA 94133

In collaboration with Williams-Sonoma
3250 Van Ness Avenue, San Francisco, CA 94109

Production by Mandarin Offset, Hong Kong
Printed in China

CONTENTS

Risotto Basics

THE PLEASURES OF RISOTTO AND RICE DISHES

Considering the fact that half of the world's population relies on it as their major source of sustenance, rice—not bread—deserves pride of place as the true staff of life. Archaeological evidence suggests that the grain, which most likely originated in India, was cultivated in the Yangtze Delta of China at least 7,000 years ago. Alexander the Great is said to have brought it to the Mediterranean in the fourth century B.C., where it spread across Europe and to the Americas.

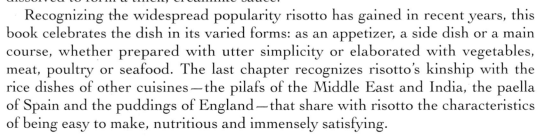

Risotto, a northern Italian specialty, may well present the staple in its most glorious form. Short, plump grains of Arborio rice are slowly simmered and stirred in hot liquid until they are chewy and tender—al dente, as they say in Italy—and their surface starch has dissolved to form a thick, creamlike sauce.

Recognizing the widespread popularity risotto has gained in recent years, this book celebrates the dish in its varied forms: as an appetizer, a side dish or a main course, whether prepared with utter simplicity or elaborated with vegetables, meat, poultry or seafood. The last chapter recognizes risotto's kinship with the rice dishes of other cuisines—the pilafs of the Middle East and India, the paella of Spain and the puddings of England—that share with risotto the characteristics of being easy to make, nutritious and immensely satisfying.

VARIETIES OF RICE

Only two species of rice have been cultivated by humankind: *Oryza glaberrima,* a species confined to West Africa, and the much more widespread *Oryza sativa,* of which approximately 120,000 different varieties are grown.

All those varieties, however, may be divided into two main types: long-grain, which are less starchy and usually cook up into the fluffy, dry, separate grains of such dishes as pilafs; and medium- or short-grain, which have extra surface starch that yields the sticky rice of Japanese cuisine and the creamy sauce of risottos.

The main type of rice used for risotto is a plump medium-grain variety known as Arborio. Two other rice hybrids can be used when making risotto: Carnaroli, prized for its firm texture; and Vialone Nano, which has shorter grains that yield a less creamy sauce and cook about 5 minutes more quickly than Arborio.

NUTRITIONAL ANALYSIS

Each recipe in this book has been evaluated by a registered dietitian. The resulting analysis lists the nutrient breakdown per serving. Use these numbers to plan nutritionally balanced meals. All ingredients listed with each recipe have been included in the analysis. Exceptions are items inserted "to taste" and those listed as "optional."

When seasoning with salt, bear in mind that each teaspoon of regular salt contains 2,200 mg of sodium. The addition of black or white pepper does not alter nutrient values. Substituted ingredients, recipe variations and accompaniments suggested in the recipe introductions or shown in the photographs have not been included in the analysis.

NUTRITIONAL TERMS

CALORIES (KILOJOULES)
Calories provide a measure of the energy provided by any given food. A calorie equals the heat energy necessary to raise the temperature of 1 kg of water by 1° Celsius. One calorie is equal to 4.2 kilojoules—a term used instead of calories in some countries.

PROTEIN
One of the basic life-giving nutrients, protein helps build and repair body tissues and performs other essential functions. One gram of protein contains 4 calories. A healthy diet derives about 15 percent of daily calories from protein.

CARBOHYDRATES
Classed as either simple (sugars) or complex (starches), carbohydrates are the main source of dietary energy. One gram contains 4 calories. A healthy diet derives about 55 percent of daily calories from carbohydrates, with not more than 10 percent coming from sugars.

TOTAL FAT
This number measures the grams of fat per serving, with 1 gram of fat equivalent to 9 calories, more than twice the calories present in a gram of protein or carbohydrate. Experts recommend that total fat intake be limited to a maximum of 30 percent of total daily calories.

SATURATED FAT
Derived from animal products and some tropical oils, saturated fat has been found to raise blood cholesterol and should be limited to no more than one-third of total daily fat calories.

CHOLESTEROL
Cholesterol is a fatty substance present in foods of animal origin. Experts suggest a daily intake of no more than 300 mg. Plant foods contain no cholesterol.

SODIUM
Derived from salt and naturally present in many foods, sodium helps maintain a proper balance of body fluids. Excess intake can lead to high blood pressure, or hypertension, in sodium-sensitive people. Those not sensitive should limit daily intake to about 2,200 mg.

FIBER
Dietary fiber aids elimination and may help prevent heart disease, intestinal disease and some forms of cancer. A healthy diet should include 20–35 grams of fiber daily.

Making Risotto

This recipe, an easy-to-follow formula for making risotto at its most basic, employs principles that apply to any risotto or similar rice dish you might wish to make. Choose a cooking vessel large and wide enough to allow for easy stirring and adequate evaporation of the cooking liquid.

Although chicken stock is the classic risotto cooking liquid, vegetable or fish stock can be substituted in basic risotto. If you have no homemade stock on hand, canned or frozen stock or bottled clam juice can be used instead. Look for low-sodium versions and be sure to taste your dish before adding salt when using commercial stocks and broths.

Cook risotto with unsalted butter, which allows greater leeway in seasoning than salted versions. Be sure to heat the butter just until it melts and do not let it burn while sautéing the onion. Yellow onions were used when designing and testing the recipes in this book, but any kind of onion can be used to make risotto. Allow the onion to cook for the full time listed in the recipes. Slow cooking over moderate heat gives onions a gentle, sweet flavor. You want the onion to be flavorful and translucent, not browned, before adding the rice.

Any dry white wine fit to drink can be used in risotto. Never cook with wine that has soured as that flavor will be absorbed into the rice. Most of the alcohol will evaporate during the simmering. To get the most flavor from the Parmesan cheese, freshly grate it just before adding it to the dish.

Perfectly made risotto will be quite creamy. If it cooks too fast or sits too long after cooking it may become dry. If that happens, add more liquid, stirring constantly, to bring the rice to a creamy consistency.

Classic Risotto

To make a perfect risotto in the classic style, be sure to do the following: Use imported Arborio rice; once the grains are coated with butter, add the hot liquid a little at a time; adjust the heat so that the liquid simmers actively and stir the mixture almost constantly. Toward the end of the cooking time, the rice should be checked to see if it is al dente: tender but still firm and chewy.

6   cups (48 fl oz/1.5 l) Chicken Stock *(recipe on page 127)*

2   tablespoons unsalted butter

1   onion, chopped

2½ cups (17½ oz/545 g) Arborio or medium-grain rice

⅔   cup (5 fl oz/160 ml) dry white wine

1¾ cups (7 oz/220 g) freshly grated Parmesan cheese

Salt and freshly ground pepper

Makes 6 cups (30 oz/930 g)

MAKING CLASSIC RISOTTO: STEP-BY-STEP

1. SIMMERING THE STOCK
In a small saucepan over high heat, bring the Chicken Stock to a simmer. Reduce the heat to low and keep the liquid hot.

2. SAUTÉING THE ONION
In a heavy large saucepan over low heat, melt the butter. Add the onion and sauté, stirring frequently, until it is translucent, about 8 minutes.

3. ADDING RICE
Add the rice and stir until a white spot appears in the center of the grains, about 1 minute. Add the wine and stir until it is absorbed, about 2 minutes.

4. ADDING THE STOCK
Add the stock ¾ cup (6 fl oz/ 180 ml) at a time, stirring constantly, until the rice starts to soften, about 10 minutes. Use three-fourths of the stock.

5. STIRRING THE MIX
Add the remaining stock ½ cup (4 fl oz/125 ml) at a time, stirring constantly, until the rice is tender and creamy, about 10 minutes longer.

6. FINISHING THE RISOTTO
Add the Parmesan cheese and salt and pepper to taste. Stir to mix well. Remove from heat. To serve, spoon into shallow bowls or onto plates.

EASY RISOTTO

Using the same ingredients as Classic Risotto, the method explained below is slightly easier, requiring less stirring and attention. It can be used to make any of the recipes in this book. Risottos made by this method will have the same flavor as those following the Classic steps but will be slightly less creamy.

1. Begin making Easy Risotto using the same method of simmering the stock and sautéing the onion as described in Steps 1 and 2 at left.
2. Add the rice and stir until a white spot appears in the center of the grains, about 1 minute. Add the wine and stir until it is absorbed, about 2 minutes. Add three-fourths of the stock.
3. Increase the heat to high and bring to a boil. Reduce the heat and simmer, uncovered, stirring occasionally and adding the remaining liquid by ¼ cupfuls (2 fl oz/60 ml) as the mixture thickens, until the rice is just tender but still slightly firm in the center and the mixture is creamy, about 20 minutes.
4. Finish the risotto as described in Step 6 at left, by adding Parmesan cheese and salt and pepper to taste and stirring to mix well.

FLAVORING RISOTTO

Once you have mastered the basic risotto techniques demonstrated on the previous pages, you'll be able to create an incredibly varied range of dishes, simply by adding other ingredients to your risotto. Spices, fresh or dried herbs and cheeses (see page 14) each add a particular aroma and flavor.

A GUIDE TO SPICES

From exotic saffron to basic black pepper, spices provide a range of flavors in risotto recipes. To maintain their freshness, store spices in a tightly covered container in a cool, dark place and use within 6 months of purchase.

CUMIN A Middle Eastern spice with a strong, dusky, aromatic flavor. Cumin is sold ground or as small seeds.

FENNEL SEEDS The small crescent-shaped seeds of the fennel plant are prized for their mild anise flavor.

GINGER The sweet, strongly flavored rhizome of the tropical ginger plant is sold either fresh or dried and ground.

PAPRIKA Derived from the dried paprika pepper, this powdered spice is available in sweet, mild and hot forms. Hungarian paprika is the best, but Spanish paprika, which is more mild, may also be used.

PEPPER Pungent black peppercorns are slightly underripe pepper berries, whose hulls oxidize as they dry. Milder white peppercorns come from fully ripened berries, with the husks removed before drying. Pepper is best purchased as whole peppercorns, to be ground in a pepper mill as needed.

RED PEPPER FLAKES The coarsely crushed flakes of dried red chilies, including the seeds, add a moderately hot seasoning to foods.

SAFFRON This expensive but intensely aromatic, golden spice is made from the dried stigmas of a species of crocus. It is sold either as threads—the dried stigmas—or in powdered form.

SALT The most common culinary seasoning in the world is best added to recipes at the cook's discretion, "to taste." Common table salt is fine grained and is supplemented with iodine. For extra flavor use kosher salt, which is slightly coarser, is made without anti-caking additives and imparts more flavor than refined table salt.

A GUIDE TO HERBS

Culinary herbs add great flavor and visual appeal to risotto and other rice dishes and provide an excellent alternative to salt. Keep fresh herbs in water—as you would cut flowers—awaiting use. They will last up to 1 week, if trimmed daily and stored in the refrigerator. Store dried herbs in a tightly covered container in a cool, dark place and use within 6 months.

ARUGULA

BASIL

CHIVES

DILL

FENNEL

OREGANO

FLAT-LEAF
PARSLEY

MINT

MARJORAM

SAGE

ROSEMARY

TARRAGON

THYME

A GUIDE TO CHEESES

The following cheeses are used in this book to enrich and flavor risotto and other rice dishes. Look for them and other cheeses at well-stocked food stores or at specialty or ethnic markets.

Cheeses cannot be used interchangeably in recipes. Differences in fat and moisture content cause them to react differently when heated. If the cheese called for in a particular recipe is not available, substitute a cheese with a similar fat and moisture content.

After adding the cheese, do not cook the risotto or rice too long. Stir in the cheese just until it melts. Prolonged cooking causes the casein in cheese to coagulate and separate from the water and fat, producing a stringy consistency and giving the rice an oily surface.

Store cheeses wrapped in plastic wrap in the refrigerator. Changing the wrap every few days lengthens the storage time to several weeks.

FONTINA A semi-firm, creamy, delicate cheese with a slightly nutty taste, made from cow's milk. Make sure to buy genuine Italian Fontina, which comes from the Aosta Valley of northwestern Italy; it is superior to Fontina from other countries.

GOAT CHEESE Cheeses made from goat's milk may be fresh, mild and white, or aged, ivory in color, and more sharply flavored. Sold shaped into small rounds or logs, either kind may be coated with pepper, ash or a mixture of herbs, which mildly flavors the cheese. Goat cheeses are also known by the French term chèvre.

GORGONZOLA A creamy, blue-veined Italian cheese. Other creamy blue cheeses may be substituted.

GOUDA A semi-soft, rich variety of Dutch cheese, yellowish in color and with a flavor ranging from mild to strong. Gouda is similar to Edam.

MOZZARELLA A rindless white, mild-tasting Italian variety of cheese traditionally made from water buffalo's milk and sold fresh. Commercially produced and packaged cow's milk mozzarella is now much more common, although it has less flavor. Look for fresh mozzarella sold immersed in water. Mozzarella is also sometimes smoked, yielding a firmer-textured, aromatic but still mild cheese.

PARMESAN A firm cheese made from half skimmed and half whole cow's milk, its sharp, salty flavor results from up to two years of aging. In its prime, a good piece of Parmesan cheese is dry but not grainy and flakes easily. For the best flavor in recipes, buy imported Italian Parmesan in block form and grate as needed.

PECORINO Italian sheep's milk cheese, sold either fresh or aged. Two of its most popular aged forms are pecorino romano and pecorino sardo; the latter cheese is tangier than the former.

$\mathscr{S}$HAPING RISOTTO

Included in this book are recipes that highlight another appealing quality of rice: the fact that leftovers that can be molded into supplì (recipe on page 103) or croquettes (recipe on page 99), yielding appetizers so easily made and delicious that you might be tempted to prepare a batch of risotto for that express purpose.

MAKING SUPPLÌ: STEP-BY-STEP

1. COMBINING INGREDIENTS
Combine the cooked risotto and lightly beaten eggs. Place the bread crumbs in a cake pan.

2. ADDING THE FILLING
Drop 1 tablespoon of the mixture onto the bread crumbs and press into it the filling—here, cheese and porcini.

3. FORMING THE SUPPLÌ
Top with another 1 tablespoon of the risotto mixture. Using your hands, gently form into a cylinder.

4. COATING AND CHILLING
Coat with the bread crumbs. Place on a waxed-paper-lined baking sheet and chill in the refrigerator for at least 1 hour.

5. DEEP-FRYING
In a large saucepan, in batches, deep-fry in 350°F (180°C) oil turning occasionally, until golden brown, about 3 minutes.

6. SERVING THE SUPPLÌ
Drain the supplì on paper towels and keep warm in a 250°F (120°C) oven while preparing the remainder.

Appetizers

RISOTTO WITH RED BELL PEPPER, TOMATO, MINT AND FETA

Seek out a not-too-salty variety of feta cheese that won't overwhelm the other flavors in a zesty combination that makes an excellent first course before lamb or seafood. Substitute yellow bell pepper (capsicum) for the red, if you like.

5½ cups (44 fl oz/1.4 l) Chicken or Vegetable Stock *(recipes on pages 126–127)*

2 tablespoons olive oil

1 onion, chopped

1 large red bell pepper (capsicum), stemmed, seeded, deribbed and cut into ½-inch (12-mm) pieces *(see page 124)*

1½ cups (10½ oz/330 g) Arborio or medium-grain rice

2 tomatoes, seeded and chopped *(see page 125)*

¾ cup (4 oz/125 g) crumbled feta cheese

¼ cup (⅓ oz/10 g) finely chopped fresh mint

Salt and freshly ground pepper

Fresh mint leaves

1. In a small saucepan over high heat, bring the Chicken or Vegetable Stock to a boil. Reduce the heat to low and keep the liquid hot.

2. In a heavy medium saucepan over medium-low heat, heat the olive oil and sauté the onion, stirring frequently, until it begins to soften, about 5 minutes. Add the bell pepper and sauté, stirring frequently, until the pepper begins to soften, about 5 minutes.

3. To the onion mixture, add the rice and stir until a white spot appears in the center of the grains, about 1 minute. Add ¾ cup (6 fl oz/180 ml) of the stock, adjust the heat to simmer, if needed, so that the liquid bubbles and is absorbed slowly. Stir until the liquid is absorbed. Continue cooking, adding the liquid ¾ cup (6 fl oz/180 ml) at a time and stirring almost constantly, until the rice starts to soften, about 10 minutes.

4. Add the tomatoes. Continue cooking, adding the liquid ½ cup (4 fl oz/125 ml) at a time and stirring almost constantly, until the rice is just tender but slightly firm in the center and the mixture is creamy, about 10 minutes longer.

5. Add the feta cheese, mint and salt and pepper to taste. Stir to mix well.

6. To serve, spoon into shallow bowls or onto plates. Garnish with the mint leaves.

Serves 6

NUTRITIONAL ANALYSIS: Calories 316 (Kilojoules 1,328); Protein 10 g; Carbohydrates 47 g; Total Fat 11 g; Saturated Fat 4 g; Cholesterol 17 mg; Sodium 322 mg; Dietary Fiber 2 g

 ASPARAGUS RISOTTO

Prepare this dish when springtime asparagus is at its best. If you wish, substitute another herb for the tarragon, such as chervil or dill. A little grated lemon zest also nicely complements the vegetable.

5½ cups (44 fl oz/1.4 l) Chicken or Vegetable Stock *(recipes on pages 126–127)*

1¼ lb (625 g) asparagus, cut into 1½-inch (4-cm) lengths

¾ cup (6 fl oz/180 ml) dry white wine

2 tablespoons olive oil

1 onion, chopped

2 cups (14 oz/440 g) Arborio or medium-grain rice

1 cup (4 oz/125 g) freshly grated Parmesan cheese

1 tablespoon finely chopped fresh tarragon or 1 teaspoon dried

Salt and freshly ground pepper

Fresh tarragon sprigs

1. In a small saucepan over high heat, bring the Chicken or Vegetable Stock to a boil. Add the asparagus and boil until just tender-crisp, about 2 minutes. Using a slotted spoon, transfer the asparagus to a bowl and set aside.
2. Add the wine to the stock and bring to a simmer. Reduce the heat to low and keep the liquid hot.
3. In a heavy large saucepan over medium-low heat, heat the olive oil and sauté the onion, stirring frequently, until it is translucent, about 8 minutes.
4. To the onion, add the rice and stir until a white spot appears in the center of the grains, about 1 minute. Add ¾ cup (6 fl oz/180 ml) of the stock, adjust the heat to simmer, if needed, so that the liquid bubbles and is absorbed slowly. Stir until the liquid is absorbed. Continue cooking, adding the liquid ¾ cup (6 fl oz/180 ml) at a time and stirring almost constantly, until the rice starts to soften, about 10 minutes. Continue cooking, adding the liquid ½ cup (4 fl oz/125 ml) at a time and stirring almost constantly, until the rice is just tender but slightly firm in the center and the mixture is creamy, about 10 minutes longer.
5. Add the asparagus, Parmesan cheese, chopped tarragon and salt and pepper to taste. Stir to mix well.
6. To serve, spoon into shallow bowls or onto plates. Garnish with the tarragon sprigs.

Serves 6

NUTRITIONAL ANALYSIS: Calories 409 (Kilojoules 1,718); Protein 17 g; Carbohydrates 61 g; Total Fat 12 g; Saturated Fat 5 g; Cholesterol 13 mg; Sodium 413 mg; Dietary Fiber 2 g

Appetizers

RED WINE AND PARMESAN RISOTTO

This risotto gains vibrant color and pungent flavor from the red wine used as part of its cooking liquid, making the dish an excellent choice before a beef or veal main course. For the best flavor, choose a full-bodied wine.

4 cups (32 fl oz/1 l) Chicken or Vegetable Stock *(recipes on pages 126–127)*

2 cups (16 fl oz/500 ml) dry red wine

3 tablespoons unsalted butter

1 onion, chopped

2 cups (14 oz/440 g) Arborio or medium-grain rice

1 cup (4 oz/125 g) freshly grated Parmesan cheese

Salt and freshly ground pepper

Finely chopped fresh flat-leaf (Italian) parsley

Fresh flat-leaf (Italian) parsley leaves

1. In a small saucepan over high heat, combine the Chicken or Vegetable Stock and wine and bring to a simmer. Reduce the heat to low and keep the liquid hot.
2. In a heavy medium saucepan over medium-low heat, melt 2 tablespoons of the butter and sauté the onion, stirring frequently, until it is translucent, about 8 minutes.
3. To the onion, add the rice and stir until a white spot appears in the center of the grains, about 1 minute. Add ¾ cup (6 fl oz/180 ml) of the stock, adjust the heat to simmer, if needed, so that the liquid bubbles and is absorbed slowly. Stir until the liquid is absorbed. Continue cooking, adding the liquid ¾ cup (6 fl oz/180 ml) at a time and stirring almost constantly, until the rice starts to soften, about 10 minutes. Continue cooking, adding the liquid ½ cup (4 fl oz/125 ml) at a time and stirring almost constantly, until the rice is just tender but slightly firm in the center and the mixture is creamy, about 10 minutes longer.
4. Add the Parmesan cheese, the remaining 1 tablespoon butter and salt and pepper to taste. Stir to mix well.
5. To serve, spoon into shallow bowls or onto plates. Garnish with the chopped parsley and parsley leaves.

Serves 6

NUTRITIONAL ANALYSIS: Calories 422 (Kilojoules 1,773); Protein 14 g; Carbohydrates 58 g; Total Fat 13 g; Saturated Fat 7 g; Cholesterol 28 mg; Sodium 386 mg; Dietary Fiber 1 g

GORGONZOLA RISOTTO WITH TOMATO TOPPING

If you can't find Gorgonzola, substitute Danish blue or another blue-veined cheese. For another effect, the tomato topping may also be stirred into the risotto just before serving.

3 tomatoes, seeded and chopped *(see page 125)*

1 cup (3 oz/90 g) chopped green (spring) onions, green and white parts (about 9)

3 tablespoons olive oil

1½ teaspoons balsamic vinegar

5½ cups (44 fl oz/1.4 l) Chicken or Vegetable Stock *(recipes on pages 126–127)*

1½ cups (10½ oz/330 g) Arborio or medium-grain rice

½ cup (2½ oz/75 g) crumbled Gorgonzola cheese

Salt and freshly ground pepper

1. To make the tomato topping, in a medium bowl, mix the tomatoes, ¼ cup (¾ oz/20 g) of the green onions, 1½ tablespoons of the olive oil and the vinegar.

2. In a small saucepan over high heat, bring the Chicken or Vegetable Stock to a simmer. Reduce the heat to low and keep the liquid hot.

3. In a heavy medium saucepan over medium-low heat, heat the remaining 1½ tablespoons olive oil. Add ½ cup (1½ oz/45 g) of the green onions and stir for 2 minutes.

4. To the green onions, add the rice and stir until a white spot appears in the center of the grains, about 1 minute. Add ¾ cup (6 fl oz/180 ml) of the stock, adjust the heat to simmer, if needed, so that the liquid bubbles and is absorbed slowly. Stir until the liquid is absorbed. Continue cooking, adding the liquid ¾ cup (6 fl oz/180 ml) at a time and stirring almost constantly, until the rice starts to soften, about 10 minutes. Continue cooking, adding the liquid ½ cup (4 fl oz/125 ml) at a time and stirring almost constantly, until the rice is just tender but slightly firm in the center and the mixture is creamy, about 10 minutes longer.

5. Add the remaining ¼ cup (¾ oz/20 g) green onions, Gorgonzola cheese and salt and pepper to taste. Stir to mix well.

6. To serve, spoon into shallow bowls or onto plates. Top each with an equal amount of the tomato topping.

Serves 6

NUTRITIONAL ANALYSIS: Calories 321 (Kilojoules 1,348); Protein 10 g; Carbohydrates 45 g; Total Fat 13 g; Saturated Fat 4 g; Cholesterol 10 mg; Sodium 276 mg; Dietary Fiber 2 g

Appetizers

$\mathscr{P}$ORCINI, CARAMELIZED ONION AND SAGE RISOTTO

The earthiness of Italy's beloved dried porcini mushrooms, the sweetness of onions and the sharp perfume of sage add up to a classic first course. Other dried mushrooms may be substituted for the porcini.

¾ oz (20 g) dried porcini mushrooms

1 cup (8 fl oz/250 ml) hot water

5½ cups (44 fl oz/1.4 l) Chicken or Vegetable Stock *(recipes on pages 126–127)*

2 tablespoons unsalted butter

2 tablespoons olive oil

2 onions, quartered lengthwise and sliced crosswise

2 cups (14 oz/440 g) Arborio or medium-grain rice

¾ cup (6 fl oz/180 ml) dry white wine

1 tablespoon finely chopped fresh sage or 1 teaspoon dried

1½ cups (6 oz/185 g) freshly grated Parmesan cheese

Salt and freshly ground pepper

Fresh sage leaves

1. In a small bowl, combine the mushrooms and hot water. Soak for 30 minutes to soften. Drain the mushrooms, reserving the soaking liquid. Chop the mushrooms.

2. In a small saucepan over high heat, bring the Chicken or Vegetable Stock to a simmer. Reduce the heat to low and keep the liquid hot.

3. In a heavy medium saucepan over medium-high heat, melt the butter with the olive oil and sauté the onions, stirring frequently, until brown, about 10 minutes.

4. To the onions, add the rice and mushrooms and stir until a white spot appears in the center of the grains, about 1 minute. Add the wine and stir until it is absorbed, about 2 minutes. Add the chopped sage, reserved mushroom soaking liquid (discarding any sediment at the bottom) and ¾ cup (6 fl oz/180 ml) of the stock. Adjust the heat to simmer, if needed, so that the liquid bubbles and is absorbed slowly. Stir until the liquid is absorbed. Continue cooking, adding the liquid ¾ cup (6 fl oz/ 180 ml) at a time and stirring almost constantly, until the rice starts to soften, about 10 minutes. Continue cooking, adding the liquid ½ cup (4 fl oz/125 ml) at a time and stirring almost constantly, until the rice is just tender but slightly firm in the center and the mixture is creamy, about 10 minutes longer.

5. Add the Parmesan cheese and salt and pepper to taste. Stir to mix well.

6. To serve, spoon into a shallow serving bowl. Garnish with the sage leaves.

Serves 6

NUTRITIONAL ANALYSIS: Calories 479 (Kilojoules 2,014); Protein 19 g; Carbohydrates 63 g; Total Fat 18 g; Saturated Fat 8 g; Cholesterol 30 mg; Sodium 565 mg; Dietary Fiber 2 g

OZZARELLA AND DRIED TOMATO RISOTTO

The mozzarella cheese, especially if you use the fresh variety, will melt into threads, giving this risotto an intriguing texture. If you use oil-free, vacuum-packed dried tomatoes, soften them in hot water to cover before chopping.

5½ cups (44 fl oz/1.4 l) Chicken or Vegetable Stock *(recipes on pages 126–127)*

⅓ cup (3 oz/90 g) oil-packed sun-dried tomatoes

1 onion, chopped

2 cups (14 oz/440 g) Arborio or medium-grain rice

1 cup (4 oz/125 g) finely shredded mozzarella cheese (preferably fresh, packed in water)

1 cup (4 oz/125 g) freshly grated Parmesan cheese

¼ cup (⅓ oz/10 g) finely chopped fresh basil

Salt and freshly ground pepper

Basil leaves

1. In a small saucepan over high heat, bring the Chicken or Vegetable Stock to a simmer. Reduce the heat to low and keep the liquid hot.

2. Drain the sun-dried tomatoes and reserve the oil. Add more oil from the jar to equal 4 tablespoons (2 fl oz/60 ml). Chop the sun-dried tomatoes and set aside.

3. In a heavy medium saucepan over medium-low heat, heat 2 tablespoons of the oil and sauté the onion, stirring frequently, until it is translucent, about 8 minutes.

4. To the onion, add the rice and stir until a white spot appears in the center of the grains, about 1 minute. Add ¾ cup (6 fl oz/180 ml) of the stock, adjust the heat to simmer, if needed, so that the liquid bubbles and is absorbed slowly. Stir until the liquid is absorbed. Continue cooking, adding the liquid ¾ cup (6 fl oz/180 ml) at a time and stirring almost constantly, until the rice starts to soften, about 10 minutes. Continue cooking, adding the liquid ½ cup (4 fl oz/125 ml) at a time and stirring almost constantly, until the rice is just tender but slightly firm in the center and the mixture is creamy, about 10 minutes longer.

5. Add the mozzarella cheese, Parmesan cheese, sun-dried tomatoes, chopped basil, remaining 2 tablespoons oil and salt and pepper to taste. Stir to mix well.

6. To serve, spoon into shallow bowls or onto plates. Garnish with the basil leaves.

Serves 6

NUTRITIONAL ANALYSIS: Calories 529 (Kilojoules 2,220); Protein 18 g; Carbohydrates 60 g; Total Fat 25 g; Saturated Fat 6 g; Cholesterol 26 mg; Sodium 571 mg; Dietary Fiber 1 g

RISOTTO WITH GREENS, GORGONZOLA AND WALNUTS

The combination of robust greens, tangy cheese and toasted nuts makes this an ideal prelude to simple roast poultry meat. Substitute Roquefort, Danish blue or another blue-veined cheese for the Gorgonzola.

5 cups (40 fl oz/1.25 l) Chicken or Vegetable Stock *(recipes on pages 126–127)*

3 tablespoons olive oil

½ large onion, chopped

1½ cups (10½ oz/330 g) Arborio or medium-grain rice

½ cup (4 fl oz/125 ml) dry white wine

3 cups (6 oz/180 g) thinly sliced greens such as escarole, Swiss chard (silverbeet), kale or beet

¾ cup (4 oz/125 g) crumbled Gorgonzola cheese

½ cup (2 oz/60 g) walnuts, toasted and coarsely chopped *(see page 123)*

Salt and freshly ground pepper

1. In a small saucepan over high heat, bring the Chicken or Vegetable Stock to a simmer. Reduce the heat to low and keep the liquid hot.

2. In a heavy medium saucepan over medium-low heat, heat the olive oil and sauté the onion, stirring frequently, until it is translucent, about 8 minutes.

3. To the onion, add the rice and stir until a white spot appears in the center of the grains, about 1 minute. Add the wine and stir until it is absorbed, about 2 minutes. Add ¾ cup (6 fl oz/180 ml) of the stock, adjust the heat to simmer, if needed, so that the liquid bubbles and is absorbed slowly. Stir until the liquid is absorbed. Continue cooking, adding the liquid ¾ cup (6 fl oz/180 ml) at a time and stirring almost constantly, until the rice starts to soften, about 10 minutes.

4. Add the greens and continue cooking, adding the liquid ½ cup (4 fl oz/125 ml) at a time and stirring almost constantly, until the rice is just tender but slightly firm in the center and the mixture is creamy, about 10 minutes longer.

5. Add the Gorgonzola cheese, walnuts and salt and pepper to taste. Stir to mix well.

6. To serve, spoon into shallow bowls or onto plates.

Serves 6

NUTRITIONAL ANALYSIS: Calories 402 (Kilojoules 1,688); Protein 12 g; Carbohydrates 46 g; Total Fat 21 g; Saturated Fat 6 g; Cholesterol 17 mg; Sodium 375 mg; Dietary Fiber 2 g

$\mathscr{F}$RESH HERB AND PARMESAN RISOTTO

Simple and pure, this recipe benefits greatly from being made with the best Parmesan cheese available. Serve it before an equally straightforward main course such as roast chicken or grilled fish.

5 cups (40 fl oz/1.25 l) Chicken or Vegetable Stock *(recipes on pages 126–127)*

3 tablespoons olive oil

½ large onion, chopped

1½ cups (10½ oz/330 g) Arborio or medium-grain rice

½ cup (4 fl oz/125 ml) dry white wine

¾ cup (3 oz/90 g) freshly grated Parmesan cheese plus additional freshly grated Parmesan cheese

⅓ cup (½ oz/15 g) finely chopped mixed fresh herbs such as basil, arugula, chives and flat-leaf (Italian) parsley

Salt and freshly ground pepper

1. In a small saucepan over high heat, bring the Chicken or Vegetable Stock to a simmer. Reduce the heat to low and keep the liquid hot.

2. In a heavy medium saucepan over medium-low heat, heat the olive oil and sauté the onion, stirring frequently, until it is translucent, about 8 minutes.

3. To the onion, add the rice and stir until a white spot appears in the center of the grains, about 1 minute. Add the wine and stir until it is absorbed, about 2 minutes. Add ¾ cup (6 fl oz/180 ml) of the stock, adjust the heat to simmer, if needed, so that the liquid bubbles and is absorbed slowly. Stir until the liquid is absorbed. Continue cooking, adding the liquid ¾ cup (6 fl oz/180 ml) at a time and stirring almost constantly, until the rice starts to soften, about 10 minutes. Continue cooking, adding the liquid ½ cup (4 fl oz/125 ml) at a time and stirring almost constantly, until the rice is just tender but slightly firm in the center and the mixture is creamy, about 10 minutes longer.

4. Add the ¾ cup (3 oz/90 g) Parmesan cheese, herbs and salt and pepper to taste. Stir to mix well.

5. To serve, spoon into shallow bowls or onto plates. Pass the additional Parmesan cheese separately.

Serves 6

Nutritional Analysis: Calories 324 (Kilojoules 1,360); Protein 11 g; Carbohydrates 43 g; Total Fat 13 g; Saturated Fat 4 g; Cholesterol 10 mg; Sodium 326 mg; Dietary Fiber 1 g

RED AND YELLOW BELL PEPPER RISOTTO WITH FONTINA CHEESE

Here is a rich-tasting starter that would be good before a main course of roast chicken. For another variation on the same recipe, try using Gouda cheese in place of the Fontina.

5 cups (40 fl oz/1.25 l) Chicken or Vegetable Stock *(recipes on pages 126–127)*

2 tablespoons olive oil

1 large onion, chopped

1 *each* red and yellow bell pepper (capsicum), stemmed, seeded, deribbed and cut into ¹/₂-inch (12-mm) cubes *(see page 124)*

1 garlic clove, peeled and minced

1¹/₂ cups (10¹/₂ oz/330 g) Arborio or medium-grain rice

³/₄ cup (3 oz/90 g) grated Fontina cheese

1 tablespoon chopped fresh thyme or 1 teaspoon dried

Salt and freshly ground pepper

1. In a small saucepan over high heat, bring the Chicken or Vegetable Stock to a simmer. Reduce the heat to low and keep the liquid hot.

2. In a heavy medium saucepan over medium-low heat, heat the olive oil and sauté the onion, stirring frequently, until it begins to soften, about 5 minutes. Add the bell peppers and garlic and sauté, stirring frequently, until the peppers begin to soften, about 5 minutes.

3. To the onion mixture, add the rice and stir until a white spot appears in the center of the grains, about 1 minute. Add ³/₄ cup (6 fl oz/180 ml) of the stock, adjust the heat to simmer, if needed, so that the liquid bubbles and is absorbed slowly. Stir until the liquid is absorbed. Continue cooking, adding the liquid ³/₄ cup (6 fl oz/180 ml) at a time and stirring almost constantly, until the rice starts to soften, about 10 minutes. Continue cooking, adding the liquid ¹/₂ cup (4 fl oz/125 ml) at a time and stirring almost constantly, until the rice is just tender but slightly firm in the center and the mixture is creamy, about 10 minutes longer.

4. Add the Fontina cheese and thyme and stir until the cheese melts. Add the salt and pepper to taste. Stir to mix well.

5. To serve, spoon into shallow bowls or onto plates.

Serves 6

NUTRITIONAL ANALYSIS: Calories 317 (Kilojoules 1,333); Protein 10 g; Carbohydrates 46 g; Total Fat 11 g; Saturated Fat 4 g; Cholesterol 16 mg; Sodium 212 mg; Dietary Fiber 2 g

 PEA, TARRAGON AND GOAT CHEESE RISOTTO

A contemporary version of the Venetian specialty known as risi e bisi, *a cross between risotto and soup, this recipe replaces the traditional Parmesan with goat cheese and cooks the dish to a slightly thicker consistency.*

5½ cups (44 fl oz/1.4 l) Chicken or Vegetable Stock *(recipes on pages 126–127)*

3 tablespoons olive oil

½ large onion, chopped

1½ cups (10½ oz/330 g) Arborio or medium-grain rice

½ cup (4 fl oz/125 ml) dry white wine

1½ cups (7½ oz/235 g) shelled fresh peas *(see page 124)* or frozen peas

2 teaspoons finely chopped fresh tarragon or ¾ teaspoon dried

½ cup (2½ oz/75 g) crumbled mild goat cheese

Salt and freshly ground pepper

Fresh tarragon sprigs

1. In a small saucepan over high heat, bring the Chicken or Vegetable Stock to a simmer. Reduce the heat to low and keep the liquid hot.
2. In a heavy medium saucepan over medium-low heat, heat the olive oil and sauté the onion, stirring frequently, until it is translucent, about 8 minutes.
3. To the onion, add the rice and stir until a white spot appears in the center of the grains, about 1 minute. Add the wine and stir until absorbed, about 2 minutes. Add ¾ cup (6 fl oz/180 ml) of the stock, adjust the heat to simmer, if needed, so that the liquid bubbles and is absorbed slowly. Stir until the liquid is absorbed. Continue cooking, adding the liquid ¾ cup (6 fl oz/180 ml) at a time and stirring almost constantly, until the rice starts to soften, about 10 minutes.
4. Add the peas and chopped tarragon and continue cooking, adding the liquid ½ cup (4 fl oz/125 ml) at a time and stirring almost constantly, until the rice is just tender but slightly firm in the center and the mixture is creamy, about 10 minutes longer.
5. Add the goat cheese and stir until the cheese melts. Add the salt and pepper to taste. Stir to mix well.
6. To serve, spoon into shallow bowls or onto plates. Garnish with the tarragon sprigs.

Serves 6

NUTRITIONAL ANALYSIS: Calories 341 (Kilojoules 1,431); Protein 11 g; Carbohydrates 48 g; Total Fat 13 g; Saturated Fat 4 g; Cholesterol 9 mg; Sodium 170 mg; Dietary Fiber 2 g

Appetizers

Side Dishes

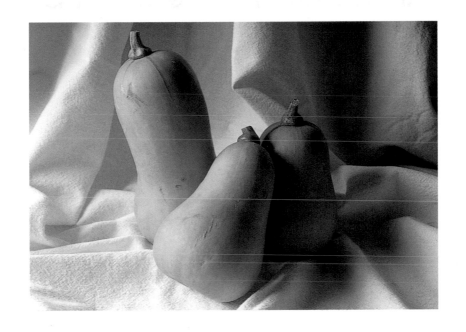

BUTTERNUT SQUASH, SAGE AND HAZELNUT RISOTTO

With its autumnal colors and flavors, this risotto is ideal served alongside a main course of grilled pork chops. If you're out of hazelnuts (filberts), use toasted blanched almonds instead.

5½ cups (44 fl oz/1.4 l) Chicken or Vegetable Stock *(recipes on pages 126–127)*

2 tablespoons unsalted butter

1 large onion, chopped

1 butternut squash or other orange-fleshed squash, peeled and cubed *(see page 125)*

5 teaspoons chopped fresh sage or 1 teaspoon dried

1½ cups (10½ oz/330 g) Arborio or medium-grain rice

½ cup (4 fl oz/125 ml) dry white wine

⅓ cup (1 oz/30 g) freshly grated Parmesan cheese

4 tablespoons (1 oz/30 g) hazelnuts (filberts), peeled, toasted and coarsely chopped *(see page 125)*

1½ teaspoons freshly ground pepper
Salt

1. In a small saucepan over high heat, bring the Chicken or Vegetable Stock to a simmer. Reduce the heat to low and keep the liquid hot.
2. In a heavy medium saucepan over low heat, melt the butter and sauté the onion, stirring frequently, until it is soft and light brown, about 10 minutes. Add the squash and 4 teaspoons of the fresh sage or all the dried sage and sauté, stirring frequently, for 2 minutes. Cover and cook until the squash is almost tender, about 6 minutes.
3. Uncover the squash pan, add the rice and stir until a white spot appears in the center of the grains, about 1 minute. Add the wine and stir until absorbed, about 2 minutes. Add ¾ cup (6 fl oz/180 ml) of the stock, adjust the heat to simmer, if needed, so that the liquid bubbles and is absorbed slowly. Stir until the liquid is absorbed. Continue cooking, adding the liquid ¾ cup (6 fl oz/180 ml) at a time and stirring almost constantly, until the rice starts to soften, about 10 minutes. Continue cooking, adding the liquid ½ cup (4 fl oz/125 ml) at a time and stirring almost constantly, until the rice is just tender but slightly firm in the center and the mixture is creamy, about 10 minutes longer.
4. Add the Parmesan cheese, 3 tablespoons of the nuts, the pepper and salt to taste. Stir to mix well.
5. To serve, spoon into a serving bowl or onto plates. Garnish with the remaining 1 teaspoon fresh sage, if using, and the remaining 1 tablespoon nuts.

Serves 6

NUTRITIONAL ANALYSIS: Calories 317 (Kilojoules 1,330); Protein 9 g; Carbohydrates 50 g; Total Fat 11 g; Saturated Fat 4 g; Cholesterol 14 mg; Sodium 186 mg; Dietary Fiber 3 g

FENNEL, LEEK AND PANCETTA RISOTTO

Three forms of fennel—the bulb vegetable, the dried seeds and the feathery fronds—add the subtly sweet flavor of anise to this risotto. If you can't find pancetta—unsmoked Italian bacon—substitute another kind of bacon.

5   cups (40 fl oz/1.25 l) Chicken or Vegetable Stock *(recipes on pages 126—127)*

2   tablespoons olive oil

2   leeks, light green and white parts, halved lengthwise and sliced crosswise *(see page 123)*

1   fennel bulb, quartered lengthwise and sliced crosswise

1½ cups (10½ oz/330 g) Arborio or medium-grain rice

4   oz (125 g) pancetta, chopped

½   teaspoon fennel seeds, crushed

¾   cup (6 fl oz/180 ml) dry white wine

½   cup (2 oz/60 g) freshly grated pecorino romano cheese plus additional freshly grated pecorino romano cheese

Salt and freshly ground pepper

Fresh fennel fronds

1. In a small saucepan over high heat, bring the Chicken or Vegetable Stock to a simmer. Reduce the heat to low and keep the liquid hot.

2. In a heavy large saucepan over low heat, heat the olive oil and sauté the leeks, stirring frequently, until they begin to soften, about 5 minutes. Add the sliced fennel and sauté, stirring frequently, until the fennel begins to soften, about 5 minutes.

3. To the leek mixture, add the rice, pancetta and fennel seeds and stir for 1 minute. Add the wine and stir until it is absorbed, about 2 minutes. Add ¾ cup (6 fl oz/180 ml) of the stock, adjust the heat to simmer, if needed, so that the liquid bubbles and is absorbed slowly. Stir until the liquid is absorbed. Continue cooking, adding the liquid ¾ cup (6 fl oz/180 ml) at a time and stirring almost constantly, until the rice starts to soften, about 10 minutes. Continue cooking, adding the liquid ½ cup (4 fl oz/125 ml) at a time and stirring almost constantly, until the rice is just tender but slightly firm in the center and the mixture is creamy, about 10 minutes longer.

4. Add the ½ cup (2 oz/60 g) pecorino romano cheese and salt and pepper to taste. Stir to mix well.

5. To serve, spoon into a serving bowl or onto plates. Garnish with the fennel fronds. Pass the additional pecorino romano cheese separately.

Serves 6

NUTRITIONAL ANALYSIS: Calories 413 (Kilojoules 1,735); Protein 11 g; Carbohydrates 48 g; Total Fat 21 g; Saturated Fat 7 g; Cholesterol 22 mg; Sodium 439 mg; Dietary Fiber 2 g

PROSCIUTTO AND RADICCHIO RISOTTO

The pairing of two classic Italian ingredients makes this side dish both simple and elegant, a perfect companion to grilled or broiled lamb. If you cannot find prosciutto, substitute another dry-cured raw ham.

5½ cups (44 fl oz/1.4 l) Chicken or Vegetable Stock *(recipes on pages 126–127)*

2 tablespoons olive oil

½ large onion, chopped

2 cups (14 oz/440 g) Arborio or medium-grain rice

¾ cup (6 fl oz/180 ml) dry white wine

9 oz (280 g) radicchio, thinly sliced

3 oz (90 g) thinly sliced prosciutto, coarsely chopped

¾ cup (3 oz/90 g) freshly grated Parmesan cheese plus additional freshly grated Parmesan cheese

Salt and freshly ground pepper

1. In a small saucepan over high heat, bring the Chicken or Vegetable Stock to a simmer. Reduce the heat to low and keep the liquid hot.

2. In a heavy medium saucepan over medium-low heat, heat the olive oil and sauté the onion, stirring frequently, until it is translucent, about 8 minutes.

3. To the onion, add the rice and stir until a white spot appears in the center of the grains, about 1 minute. Add the wine and stir until it is absorbed, about 2 minutes. Add ¾ cup (6 fl oz/180 ml) of the stock, adjust the heat to simmer, if needed, so that the liquid bubbles and is absorbed slowly. Stir until the liquid is absorbed. Continue cooking, adding the liquid ¾ cup (6 fl oz/180 ml) at a time and stirring almost constantly, until the rice starts to soften, about 10 minutes.

4. Add the radicchio and continue cooking, adding the liquid ½ cup (4 fl oz/125 ml) at a time and stirring almost constantly, until the rice is just tender but slightly firm in the center and the mixture is creamy, about 10 minutes longer.

5. Add the prosciutto, the ¾ cup (3 oz/90 g) Parmesan cheese and salt and pepper to taste. Stir to mix well.

6. To serve, spoon into a serving bowl or onto plates. Pass the additional Parmesan cheese separately.

Serves 6

NUTRITIONAL ANALYSIS: Calories 408 (Kilojoules 1,712); Protein 17 g; Carbohydrates 58 g; Total Fat 13 g; Saturated Fat 4 g; Cholesterol 21 mg; Sodium 616 mg; Dietary Fiber 2 g

ARTICHOKE RISOTTO

Using frozen artichoke hearts, widely available in well-stocked food stores, makes it possible to serve this dish at any time of year. Here, it is paired with poached salmon for a summertime feast.

5½ cups (44 fl oz/1.4 l) Chicken or Vegetable Stock *(recipes on pages 126–127)*

2   tablespoons olive oil

½   onion, chopped

1½ cups (10½ oz/330 g) Arborio or medium-grain rice

9   oz (280 g) frozen artichoke hearts, thawed and halved

1¼ cups (5 oz/155 g) freshly grated Parmesan cheese

1½ oz (45 g) thinly sliced prosciutto, chopped

½   cup (¾ oz/20 g) thinly sliced fresh basil
    Salt and freshly ground pepper
    Fresh basil leaves

1. In a small saucepan over high heat, bring the Chicken or Vegetable Stock to a simmer. Reduce the heat to low and keep the liquid hot.

2. In a heavy medium saucepan over medium-low heat, heat the olive oil and sauté the onion, stirring frequently, until it is translucent, about 8 minutes.

3. To the onion, add the rice and stir until a white spot appears in the center of the grains, about 1 minute. Add ¾ cup (6 fl oz/180 ml) of the stock, adjust the heat to simmer, if needed, so that the liquid bubbles and is absorbed slowly. Stir until the liquid is absorbed. Continue cooking, adding the liquid ¾ cup (6 fl oz/180 ml) at a time and stirring almost constantly, until the rice starts to soften, about 10 minutes.

4. Add the artichoke hearts and continue cooking, adding the liquid ½ cup (4 fl oz/125 ml) at a time and stirring almost constantly, until the rice is just tender but slightly firm in the center and the mixture is creamy, about 10 minutes longer.

5. Add the Parmesan cheese, prosciutto, sliced basil and salt and pepper to taste. Stir to mix well.

6. To serve, spoon into a serving bowl or onto plates. Garnish with the basil leaves.

Serves 6

NUTRITIONAL ANALYSIS: Calories 376 (Kilojoules 1,580); Protein 18 g; Carbohydrates 47 g; Total Fat 14 g; Saturated Fat 6 g; Cholesterol 22 mg; Sodium 636 mg; Dietary Fiber 3 g

Side Dishes

$\mathcal{S}$AFFRON RISOTTO

The classic risotto alla milanese *is an easily prepared, golden, aromatic dish traditionally served in Italy with osso buco (braised veal shanks). You'll find, though, that it enhances any meal.*

5½ cups (44 fl oz/1.4 l) Chicken or Vegetable Stock *(recipes on pages 126–127)*

½ teaspoon saffron threads

4 tablespoons (2 oz/60 g) unsalted butter

½ onion, chopped

2 cups (14 oz/440 g) Arborio or medium-grain rice

¾ cup (6 fl oz/180 ml) dry white wine

¾ cup (3 oz/90 g) freshly grated Parmesan cheese

Salt and freshly ground pepper

1. In a small saucepan over high heat, bring the Chicken or Vegetable Stock to a simmer. Reduce the heat to low, add the saffron and keep the liquid hot.

2. In a heavy large saucepan over medium-low heat, melt 2 tablespoons of the butter and sauté the onion, stirring frequently, until it is translucent, about 8 minutes.

3. To the onion, add the rice and stir until a white spot appears in the center of the grains, about 1 minute. Add the wine and stir until it is absorbed, about 2 minutes. Add ¾ cup (6 fl oz/180 ml) of the stock, adjust the heat to simmer, if needed, so that the liquid bubbles and is absorbed slowly. Stir until the liquid is absorbed. Continue cooking, adding the liquid ¾ cup (6 fl oz/180 ml) at a time and stirring almost constantly, until the rice starts to soften, about 10 minutes. Continue cooking, adding the liquid ½ cup (4 fl oz/125 ml) at a time and stirring almost constantly, until the rice is just tender but slightly firm in the center and the mixture is creamy, about 10 minutes longer.

4. Add the Parmesan cheese, remaining 2 tablespoons butter and salt and pepper to taste. Stir to mix well.

5. To serve, spoon into a serving bowl or onto plates.

Serves 6

NUTRITIONAL ANALYSIS: Calories 392 (Kilojoules 1,645); Protein 13 g; Carbohydrates 56 g; Total Fat 14 g; Saturated Fat 8 g; Cholesterol 30 mg; Sodium 336 mg; Dietary Fiber 1 g

ZESTY ZUCCHINI AND BASIL RISOTTO

Lemon zest and juice contribute a fresh, bright flavor to this risotto. Any leftovers can be thinned with additional Chicken or Vegetable Stock, transforming the risotto into a lovely soup. This is delicious paired with shrimp (prawns).

5 cups (40 fl oz/1.25 l) Chicken or Vegetable Stock *(recipes on pages 126–127)*

3 tablespoons olive oil

½ large onion, chopped

1½ cups (10½ oz/330 g) Arborio or medium-grain rice

½ cup (4 fl oz/125 ml) dry white wine

2 zucchini (courgettes), sliced lengthwise

1 cup (4 oz/125 g) freshly grated Parmesan cheese

3 tablespoons heavy (double) cream

1 teaspoon grated lemon zest *(see page 126)*

3 tablespoons fresh lemon juice

⅓ cup (½ oz/15 g) finely chopped fresh basil

Salt and freshly ground pepper

Fresh basil leaves

1. In a small saucepan over high heat, bring the Chicken or Vegetable Stock to a simmer. Reduce the heat to low and keep the liquid hot.
2. In a heavy medium saucepan over medium-low heat, heat the olive oil and sauté the onion, stirring frequently, until it is translucent, about 8 minutes.
3. To the onion, add the rice and stir until a white spot appears in the center of the grains, about 1 minute. Add the wine and stir until it is absorbed, about 2 minutes. Add ¾ cup (6 fl oz/180 ml) of the stock, adjust the heat to simmer, if needed, so that the liquid bubbles and is absorbed slowly. Stir until the liquid is absorbed. Continue cooking, adding the liquid ¾ cup (6 fl oz/180 ml) at a time and stirring almost constantly, until the rice starts to soften, about 10 minutes.
4. Add the zucchini and continue cooking, adding the liquid ½ cup (4 fl oz/125 ml) at a time and stirring almost constantly, until the rice is just tender but slightly firm in the center and the mixture is creamy, about 10 minutes longer.
5. Add the Parmesan cheese, cream, ¼ teaspoon of the lemon zest, the lemon juice, chopped basil and salt and pepper to taste. Stir to mix well.
6. To serve, spoon into shallow bowls or onto plates. Garnish with the basil leaves and remaining lemon zest.

Serves 6

NUTRITIONAL ANALYSIS: Calories 380 (Kilojoules 1,595); Protein 14 g; Carbohydrates 46 g; Total Fat 17 g; Saturated Fat 6 g; Cholesterol 23 mg; Sodium 406 mg; Dietary Fiber 1 g

Side Dishes

$\mathcal{B}$ROCCOLI RISOTTO WITH PARMESAN

You'll get the right amount of florets for this versatile side dish if you purchase about 1 lb (500 g) of broccoli, reserving the stalks for another recipe. Try substituting Gorgonzola or pecorino romano cheese for the Parmesan.

5½ cups (44 fl oz/1.4 l) Chicken or Vegetable Stock *(recipes on pages 126–127)*

2 tablespoons olive oil

1 onion, chopped

1½ cups (10½ oz/330 g) Arborio or medium-grain rice

4 cups (12 oz/375 g) broccoli florets

1 cup (4 oz/125 g) freshly grated Parmesan cheese plus additional freshly grated Parmesan cheese

Salt and freshly ground pepper

1. In a small saucepan over high heat, bring the Chicken or Vegetable Stock to a simmer. Reduce the heat to low and keep the liquid hot.

2. In a heavy medium saucepan over medium-low heat, heat the olive oil and sauté the onion, stirring frequently, until it is translucent, about 8 minutes.

3. To the onion, add the rice and stir until a white spot appears in the center of the grains, about 1 minute. Add ¾ cup (6 fl oz/180 ml) of the stock, adjust the heat to simmer, if needed, so that the liquid bubbles and is absorbed slowly. Stir until the liquid is absorbed. Continue cooking, adding the liquid ¾ cup (6 fl oz/180 ml) at a time and stirring almost constantly, until the rice starts to soften, about 10 minutes.

4. Add the broccoli and continue cooking, adding the liquid ½ cup (4 fl oz/125 ml) at a time and stirring almost constantly, until the rice is just tender but slightly firm in the center and the mixture is creamy, about 10 minutes longer.

5. Add the 1 cup (4 oz/125 g) Parmesan cheese and salt and pepper to taste. Stir to mix well.

6. To serve, spoon into a serving bowl or onto plates. Pass the additional Parmesan cheese separately.

Serves 6

NUTRITIONAL ANALYSIS: Calories 343 (Kilojoules 1,439); Protein 15 g; Carbohydrates 47 g; Total Fat 12 g; Saturated Fat 5 g; Cholesterol 13 mg; Sodium 422 mg; Dietary Fiber 3 g

$\mathcal{L}$IMA BEAN RISOTTO WITH PESTO

There's nothing fancy here, just simple ingredients that combine to make a risotto with an intriguing color and flavor. Using purchased pesto will make the recipe even easier. Serve with a grilled chicken breast, tomatoes and basil.

5½ cups (44 fl oz/1.4 l) Chicken or Vegetable Stock *(recipes on pages 126–127)*

2 tablespoons olive oil

1 onion, chopped

2½ cups (17½ oz/545 g) Arborio or medium-grain rice

⅔ cup (5 fl oz/160 ml) dry white wine

10 oz (315 g) frozen baby lima beans, thawed

½ cup (2 oz/60 g) freshly grated pecorino romano cheese

Salt and freshly ground pepper

PESTO

½ cup (¾ oz/20 g) fresh basil leaves

¼ cup (2 fl oz/60 ml) olive oil

⅓ cup (1½ oz/45 g) freshly grated Parmesan cheese

2 tablespoons pine nuts, toasted *(see page 125)*

1 garlic clove, peeled

1. Prepare the Pesto (see below).

2. In a small saucepan over high heat, bring the Chicken or Vegetable Stock to a simmer. Reduce the heat to low and keep the liquid hot.

3. In a heavy large saucepan over medium-low heat, heat the olive oil and sauté the onion, stirring frequently, until it is translucent, about 8 minutes.

4. To the onion, add the rice and stir until a white spot appears in the center of the grains, about 1 minute. Add the wine and stir until it is absorbed, about 2 minutes. Add ¾ cup (6 fl oz/180 ml) of the stock, adjust the heat to simmer, if needed, so that the liquid bubbles and is absorbed slowly. Stir until the liquid is absorbed. Continue cooking, adding the liquid ¾ cup (6 fl oz/180 ml) at a time and stirring almost constantly for 5 minutes. Add the lima beans and continue cooking, adding the liquid ½ cup (4 fl oz/125 ml) at a time and stirring almost constantly, until the rice is just tender but slightly firm in the center and the mixture is creamy, about 15 minutes longer.

5. Add the Pesto, pecorino romano cheese and salt and pepper to taste. Stir to mix well.

6. To serve, spoon into a serving bowl or onto plates.

Serves 6

PESTO

1. In the work bowl of a food processor with the metal blade or a blender, place the basil, olive oil, Parmesan cheese, pine nuts and garlic. Process until finely ground.

NUTRITIONAL ANALYSIS: Calories 600 (Kilojoules 2,521); Protein 18 g; Carbohydrates 84 g; Total Fat 23 g; Saturated Fat 6 g; Cholesterol 14 mg; Sodium 417 mg; Dietary Fiber 4 g

Side Dishes

ARUGULA RISOTTO WITH PARMESAN CHEESE

Used as both an herb and a salad green, arugula has a peppery, slightly bitter taste that adds real distinction to this very simple dish. If you can't find arugula, watercress also works well.

5½ cups (44 fl oz/1.4 l) Chicken or Vegetable Stock *(recipes on pages 126–127)*

2 tablespoons olive oil

½ large onion, chopped

2 cups (14 oz/440 g) Arborio or medium-grain rice

1½ cups (6 oz/185 g) freshly grated Parmesan cheese

1⅓ cups (2 oz/50 g) finely chopped arugula or watercress

Salt and freshly ground pepper

Arugula sprigs

1. In a small saucepan over high heat, bring the Chicken or Vegetable Stock to a simmer. Reduce the heat to low and keep the liquid hot.

2. In a heavy medium saucepan over medium-low heat, heat the olive oil and sauté the onion, stirring frequently, until it is translucent, about 8 minutes.

3. To the onion, add the rice and stir until a white spot appears in the center of the grains, about 1 minute. Add ¾ cup (6 fl oz/180 ml) of the stock, adjust the heat to simmer, if needed, so that the liquid bubbles and is absorbed slowly. Stir until the liquid is absorbed. Continue cooking, adding the liquid ¾ cup (6 fl oz/180 ml) at a time and stirring almost constantly, until the rice starts to soften, about 10 minutes. Continue cooking, adding the liquid ½ cup (4 fl oz/125 ml) at a time and stirring almost constantly, until the rice is just tender but slightly firm in the center and the mixture is creamy, about 10 minutes longer.

4. Add the Parmesan cheese, chopped arugula and salt and pepper to taste. Stir to mix well.

5. To serve, spoon into a serving bowl or onto plates. Garnish with the arugula sprigs.

Serves 6

NUTRITIONAL ANALYSIS: Calories 421 (Kilojoules 1,767); Protein 18 g; Carbohydrates 57 g; Total Fat 14 g; Saturated Fat 6 g; Cholesterol 19 mg; Sodium 565 mg; Dietary Fiber 1 g

$\mathcal{S}$HIITAKE MUSHROOM AND PEA RISOTTO PANCAKES

This is a wonderful use of any leftover risotto. Pair these delicious pancakes with a colorful mix of sautéed vegetables for a vegetarian meal. The shiitake mushrooms can be replaced with another variety.

1 cup (5 oz/155 g) shelled fresh peas
   (see page 124) or frozen peas, thawed

3 tablespoons unsalted butter

3 oz (90 g) fresh shiitake mushrooms,
   stemmed and coarsely chopped

2 cups (10 oz/315 g) Classic Risotto
   (recipe on page 10)

2 tablespoons finely chopped fresh
   tarragon or 1½ teaspoons dried

   Salt and freshly ground pepper

2 eggs, lightly beaten

1. If using fresh peas, in a medium saucepan of boiling salted water, blanch the fresh peas until tender, about 8 minutes. Drain.

2. In a large nonstick frying pan over medium heat, melt 1 tablespoon of the butter and sauté the mushrooms, tossing frequently, until they start to brown, about 3 minutes. Remove from the heat.

3. In a medium bowl, gently mix the Classic Risotto, cooked fresh or thawed frozen peas, sautéed mushrooms, tarragon and salt and pepper to taste. Gently mix in the eggs.

4. Return the large nonstick frying pan to medium heat and melt 1 tablespoon of the remaining butter. Working in batches and adding more butter as necessary, drop the risotto mixture into the pan to make 12 small pancakes. Using a spatula, gently press the risotto mixture into rounds. Fry until the pancakes are light brown on the bottom, about 4 minutes on each side.

5. To serve, transfer to a heated platter or plates.

Serves 6

NUTRITIONAL ANALYSIS: Calories 271 (Kilojoules 1,140); Protein 11 g; Carbohydrates 28 g; Total Fat 13 g; Saturated Fat 7 g; Cholesterol 97 mg; Sodium 240 mg; Dietary Fiber 2 g

Side Dishes

RISOTTO PANCAKES

Resembling small frittatas, these pancakes make excellent use of leftover risotto or start with the basic risotto on page 10, stirring in whatever fresh herbs that strike your fancy.

2 cups (10 oz/315 g) Classic Risotto *(recipe on page 10)*
1 egg, lightly beaten
2 tablespoons unsalted butter
6 tablespoons freshly grated Parmesan cheese plus
    additional freshly grated Parmesan cheese

1. In a medium bowl, gently mix the Classic Risotto and egg.
2. In a large nonstick frying pan over medium heat, melt 1 tablespoon of the butter. Working in batches and adding more butter as necessary, drop the risotto mixture into the pan to make 6 pancakes. Using a spatula, gently press the risotto mixture into rounds. Fry until the pancakes are light brown on the bottom, about 3 minutes.
3. Flip the pancakes. Sprinkle each with 1 tablespoon of the Parmesan cheese. Cover and cook until the cheese melts, about 1 minute. Uncover and continue frying until the pancakes are light brown on the bottom, about 2 minutes longer.
4. To serve, transfer to a heated platter or plates. Pass the additional Parmesan cheese separately.

Serves 6

NUTRITIONAL ANALYSIS: Calories 246 (Kilojoules 1,033); Protein 11 g; Carbohydrates 24 g; Total Fat 12 g; Saturated Fat 7 g; Cholesterol 62 mg; Sodium 341 mg; Dietary Fiber 1 g

Main Dishes

$\mathcal{B}$EEF BOLOGNESE LAYERED WITH CLASSIC RISOTTO

The bolognese sauce ordinarily served over spaghetti complements risotto in this easy recipe. For a lighter version, eliminate the pancetta, halve the butter and substitute ground turkey for the beef.

4 tablespoons (2 oz/60 g) unsalted butter

4 oz (125 g) pancetta or bacon, chopped

2 large onions, chopped

2 large carrots, peeled and chopped

1½ lb (750 g) lean ground (minced) beef

1 cup (8 fl oz/250 ml) dry red wine

2 cups (16 fl oz/500 ml) canned reduced-sodium beef broth

1½ cups (12 fl oz/375 ml) milk

8 large Roma (plum) tomatoes, peeled, seeded and chopped (*see page 125*) or 28 oz (875 g) canned tomatoes with juice

1 cup (8 fl oz/250 ml) tomato juice, if using fresh tomatoes

Salt and freshly ground pepper

1 recipe Classic Risotto (*recipe on page 10*)

½ cup (2 oz/60 g) freshly grated Parmesan cheese plus additional freshly grated Parmesan cheese

1. In a heavy large saucepan over medium heat, melt the butter. Add the pancetta or bacon, onions and carrots and sauté, stirring frequently, until the mixture begins to brown, about 10 minutes. Add the beef and cook, breaking up the meat with a fork, until it is brown, about 5 minutes.

2. Add the wine, reduce the heat and simmer until the wine is absorbed, stirring occasionally, about 5 minutes. Add the broth and simmer, stirring occasionally, until it is almost absorbed, about 15 minutes. Add the milk and simmer until it is almost evaporated, about 15 minutes.

3. Add the fresh tomatoes and tomato juice or canned tomatoes with their juice, reduce the heat to low and simmer the mixture slowly until it is very thick, stirring occasionally, about 1½ hours. Add salt and pepper to taste. Stir to mix well.

4. Prepare the Classic Risotto.

5. To serve, spoon half of the Classic Risotto into a large shallow serving bowl. Top with half of the beef mixture and sprinkle with ¼ cup (1 oz/30 g) of the Parmesan cheese. Repeat the layering. Pass the additional Parmesan cheese separately.

Serves 8

NUTRITIONAL ANALYSIS: Calories 859 (Kilojoules 3,606); Protein 39 g; Carbohydrates 69 g; Total Fat 47 g; Saturated Fat 22 g; Cholesterol 125 mg; Sodium 1,066 mg; Dietary Fiber 4 g

OSSO BUCO ON A BED OF RISOTTO

Slow simmering gives veal shanks rich, deep flavor, highlighted here by lemon zest and fresh rosemary. For a more traditional presentation, serve the osso buco with Saffron Risotto (recipe on page 48).

2	tablespoons unsalted butter
1½	large onions, chopped
2	garlic cloves, peeled and minced
	Strips of zest from 2 lemons *(see page 126)*
2	teaspoons finely chopped fresh rosemary or 1 teaspoon dried
2	bay leaves
1	teaspoon dried sage
2	tablespoons olive oil
6	center-cut veal shanks (about 12 oz/375 g each)
	Salt and freshly ground pepper
	All-purpose (plain) flour
1	cup (8 fl oz/250 ml) dry white wine
2½	cups (20 fl oz/625 ml) Chicken Stock *(recipe on page 127)*
1	recipe Classic Risotto *(recipe on page 10)*
⅓	cup (½ oz/15 g) finely chopped fresh flat-leaf (Italian) parsley
1	tablespoon grated lemon zest *(see page 126)*

1. Preheat an oven to 375°F (190°C).

2. In a heavy large dutch oven over medium heat, melt the butter and sauté the onions until they are translucent, about 8 minutes. Add half of the garlic, half of the lemon zest strips, the rosemary, bay leaves and sage. Sauté for 3 minutes. Remove the dutch oven from the heat.

3. In a heavy large frying pan over medium-high heat, heat the oil. Working in batches, season the veal with salt and pepper, coat with flour and cook until brown, about 4 minutes per side. Place the veal on top of the onions in the dutch oven.

4. Pour off and discard the drippings from the frying pan. Increase the heat to high, add the wine and bring to a boil, scraping up any browned bits. Add the wine mixture to the veal in the dutch oven. Add enough Chicken Stock to come to the top of the veal. Bring to a boil.

5. Cover the dutch oven and place in the oven. Cook, turning the veal and stirring occasionally, until the veal is tender and the sauce is creamy, about 1½ hours.

6. Prepare the Classic Risotto.

7. In a small bowl, combine the parsley, grated lemon zest and remaining garlic.

8. To serve, season the veal sauce with salt and pepper to taste. Spoon the Classic Risotto onto plates. Top with the veal and sauce. Sprinkle with the parsley mixture. Garnish with the remaining lemon zest strips.

Serves 6

NUTRITIONAL ANALYSIS: Calories 1,007 (Kilojoules 4,230); Protein 87 g; Carbohydrates 84 g; Total Fat 34 g; Saturated Fat 16 g; Cholesterol 277 mg; Sodium 891 mg; Dietary Fiber 3 g

MUSSELS, RED BELL PEPPER, CAPER AND OLIVE RISOTTO

Cooked in Fish Stock and the shellfish broth, this risotto is infused with the rich taste of the sea. If mussels are unavailable, substitute clams. Offer extra napkins and bowls to help guests eat the shellfish neatly at table.

6 cups (48 fl oz/1.5 l) Fish Stock *(recipe on page 127)*

3 tablespoons vegetable oil

1 large red (Spanish) onion, chopped

1½ large red bell peppers (capsicums), stemmed, seeded, deribbed and coarsely chopped *(see page 124)*
   Red pepper flakes

3 lb (750 g) mussels, scrubbed and debearded

3 cups (1⅓ lb/655 g) Arborio or medium-grain rice

¾ cup (6 fl oz/180 ml) dry white wine

½ cup (3½ oz/105 g) Kalamata olives, pitted and chopped

2 tablespoons capers, drained
   Salt and freshly ground pepper
   Fresh flat-leaf (Italian) parsley

1. In a small saucepan over high heat, bring the Fish Stock to a boil. Reduce the heat to low and keep the liquid hot.
2. In a heavy large dutch oven over medium-low heat, heat the vegetable oil and sauté the onion, stirring frequently, until it begins to soften, about 5 minutes. Add the bell peppers and sauté until they begin to soften, about 5 minutes. Add the pepper flakes to taste and the mussels, discarding any open mussels. Cover and cook until the mussels open, about 3 minutes. Using tongs, transfer the mussels to a bowl, discarding any that do not open. Cover and keep warm.
3. To the dutch oven, add the rice and stir over medium heat until a white spot appears in the center of the grains, about 1 minute. Add the wine and stir until it is absorbed, about 2 minutes. Add ¾ cup (6 fl oz/180 ml) of the stock, adjust the heat to simmer, if needed, so that the liquid bubbles and is absorbed slowly. Stir until the liquid is absorbed. Continue cooking, adding the liquid ¾ cup (6 fl oz/180 ml) at a time and stirring almost constantly, until the rice starts to soften, about 10 minutes. Continue cooking, adding the liquid ½ cup (4 fl oz/125 ml) at a time and stirring almost constantly, until the rice is just tender but slightly firm in the center and the mixture is creamy, about 10 minutes longer.
4. Add the olives, capers and salt and pepper to taste.
5. To serve, spoon onto plates. Top with the mussels and parsley.

Serves 6

NUTRITIONAL ANALYSIS: Calories 534 (Kilojoules 2,243); Protein 16 g; Carbohydrates 91 g; Total Fat 11 g; Saturated Fat 2 g; Cholesterol 18 mg; Sodium 728 mg; Dietary Fiber 3 g

Risotto

CHICKEN AND ASPARAGUS RISOTTO

Perfect for a springtime lunch, this risotto can also be made with baby artichoke hearts or broccoli florets. For an unusual, rich-tasting variation, try replacing the Parmesan with crumbled fresh mild goat cheese.

Grated zest from 2 lemons *(see page 126)*

1 lb (500 g) asparagus, cut into 1½-inch (4-cm) pieces

5½ cups (44 fl oz/1.4 l) Chicken Stock *(recipe on page 127)*

4 tablespoons (2 fl oz/60 ml) olive oil

1 whole chicken breast, skinned and boned (about 1 lb/500 g meat), cubed

1 onion, chopped

2½ cups (17½ oz/545 g) Arborio or medium-grain rice

2 cups (16 fl oz/500 ml) dry white wine

1 cup (4 oz/125 g) freshly grated Parmesan cheese

½ cup (¾ oz/20 g) finely chopped fresh flat-leaf (Italian) parsley

Fresh flat-leaf (Italian) parsley sprigs

Strips of zest from 1 lemon *(see page 126)*

1. In a small saucepan of boiling water, blanch the grated zest for 30 seconds. Drain. Repeat, using fresh water.
2. In a large saucepan of boiling salted water, cook the asparagus until just tender-crisp, about 5 minutes. Drain.
3. In a small saucepan over high heat, bring the Chicken Stock to a simmer. Reduce the heat to low and keep hot.
4. In a large saucepan over medium-low heat, heat 2 tablespoons of the olive oil and sauté the chicken, stirring frequently, until it is just opaque throughout, about 3 minutes. Using a slotted spoon, transfer the chicken to a plate.
5. In the same saucepan over medium-low heat, heat the remaining 2 tablespoons olive oil and sauté the onion, stirring frequently, until it is translucent, about 8 minutes.
6. To the onion, add the rice and stir until a white spot appears in the center of the grains, about 1 minute. Add the wine and stir until it is absorbed, about 2 minutes. Add ¾ cup (6 fl oz/180 ml) of the stock, adjust the heat to simmer, if needed, so that the liquid bubbles and is absorbed slowly. Stir until the liquid is absorbed. Continue cooking, adding the liquid ¾ cup (6 fl oz/180 ml) at a time and stirring almost constantly, until the rice starts to soften, about 10 minutes. Continue cooking, adding the liquid ½ cup (4 fl oz/125 ml) at a time and stirring almost constantly, until the rice is just tender but slightly firm in the center and the mixture is creamy, about 10 minutes longer.
7. Add the chicken, asparagus, half of the lemon zest, the Parmesan cheese and chopped parsley. Garnish with the chopped parsley, parsley sprigs and strips of lemon zest.

Serves 6

Nutritional Analysis: Calories 590 (Kilojoules 2,480); Protein 35 g; Carbohydrates 74 g; Total Fat 18 g; Saturated Fat 5 g; Cholesterol 57 mg; Sodium 466 mg; Dietary Fiber 3 g

Main Dishes

RISOTTO WITH SMOKED SALMON, SPINACH AND GOAT CHEESE

The fresh flavors and colors make this a winning choice for brunch or lunch, accompanied with crusty rolls and dry white wine. Avoid salt-cured lox or cold-smoked salmon, which have an oily texture.

6   cups (48 fl oz/1.5 l) Fish Stock (*recipe on page 127*)

3   tablespoons olive oil

2½   cups (17½ oz/545 g) Arborio or medium-grain rice

¾   cup (6 fl oz/180 ml) dry white wine

5   cups (10 oz/315 g) thinly sliced fresh spinach leaves

1¼   cups (6 oz/185 g) crumbled mild goat cheese

½   cup (1½ oz/45 g) chopped fresh chives or green (spring) onions, green and white parts

4   oz (125 g) smoked salmon, chopped

Salt and freshly ground pepper

Fresh chives

1. In a small saucepan over high heat, bring the Fish Stock to a simmer. Reduce the heat to low and keep the liquid hot.

2. In a heavy large saucepan over medium-low heat, heat the olive oil, add the rice and stir until a white spot appears in the center of the grains, about 1 minute. Add the wine and stir until it is absorbed, about 2 minutes. Add ¾ cup (6 fl oz/180 ml) of the stock, adjust the heat to simmer, if needed, so that the liquid bubbles and is absorbed slowly. Stir until the liquid is absorbed. Continue cooking, adding the liquid ¾ cup (6 fl oz/180 ml) at a time and stirring almost constantly for 15 minutes.

3. Add the spinach and continue cooking, adding the liquid ½ cup (4 fl oz/125 ml) at a time and stirring almost constantly, until the rice is just tender but slightly firm in the center and the mixture is creamy, about 5 minutes longer. Add the goat cheese, chives or green onions, salmon and salt and pepper to taste. Stir to mix well.

4. To serve, spoon into shallow bowls or onto plates. Garnish with the chives.

Serves 6

NUTRITIONAL ANALYSIS: Calories 505 (Kilojoules 2,123); Protein 17 g; Carbohydrates 71 g; Total Fat 17 g; Saturated Fat 7 g; Cholesterol 27 mg; Sodium 649 mg; Dietary Fiber 3 g

$\mathcal{S}$ALMON FILLETS ON ZUCCHINI RISOTTO

A bouquet of fresh basil, thyme and chive flowers adds an elegant touch to this main course that is easy to prepare. The risotto is delicious enough to serve without the grilled salmon as an appetizer or a side dish.

6   salmon fillets (about 8 oz/250 g each)

5   tablespoons olive oil

3   tablespoons balsamic vinegar

6   cups (48 fl oz/1.5 l) Fish Stock *(recipe on page 127)*

1   onion, chopped

2½ cups (17½ oz/545 g) Arborio or medium-grain rice

¾   cup (6 fl oz/180 ml) dry white wine

4   zucchini (courgettes), cubed

1   cup (1½ oz/45 g) finely chopped fresh basil

2   tablespoons unsalted butter
     Salt and freshly ground pepper

1. In a glass baking dish, place the salmon. Drizzle with 3 tablespoons of the olive oil and vinegar and marinate for 30 minutes.

2. Preheat a broiler (griller).

3. In a small saucepan over high heat, bring the Fish Stock to a simmer. Reduce the heat to low and keep the liquid hot.

4. In a heavy large saucepan over medium-low heat, heat the remaining 2 tablespoons olive oil and sauté the onion, stirring frequently, until it is translucent, about 8 minutes.

5. To the onion, add the rice and stir until a white spot appears in the center of the grains, about 1 minute. Add the wine and stir until it is absorbed, about 2 minutes. Add ¾ cup (6 fl oz/180 ml) of the stock, adjust the heat to simmer, if needed, so that the liquid bubbles and is absorbed slowly. Stir until the liquid is absorbed. Continue cooking, adding the liquid ¾ cup (6 fl oz/180 ml) at a time and stirring almost constantly, until the rice starts to soften, about 10 minutes.

6. Add the zucchini and continue cooking, adding the liquid ½ cup (4 fl oz/125 ml) at a time and stirring almost constantly, until the rice is just tender but slightly firm in the center and the mixture is creamy, about 10 minutes longer. Add half of the basil, butter and salt and pepper to taste.

7. Broil (grill) the fish until it is just opaque in the center, about 10 minutes per inch (2.5 cm) of thickness.

8. To serve, spoon the risotto onto a serving plate. Top with the salmon fillets. Garnish with the remaining basil.

Serves 6

NUTRITIONAL ANALYSIS: Calories 802 (Kilojoules 3,367); Protein 53 g; Carbohydrates 76 g; Total Fat 30 g; Saturated Fat 6 g; Cholesterol 135 mg; Sodium 423 mg; Dietary Fiber 3 g

 Main Dishes

CHICKEN LIVERS WITH PEAS ON A BED OF RISOTTO

*This casual dish is a rapid sauté of chicken livers, with a sauce —
made by deglazing the pan with Marsala wine — that mingles
with the risotto over which the sauté is served.*

1 recipe Classic Risotto *(recipe on page 10)*
2 cups (10 oz/315 g) shelled fresh peas *(see page 124)*
    or frozen peas, thawed
5 tablespoons (2½ oz/75 g) unsalted butter
4 shallots, thinly sliced
1½ lb (750 g) chicken livers, trimmed and cut into
    1-inch (2.5-cm) pieces
12 fresh sage leaves, chopped, or ½ teaspoon dried
⅔ cup (5 fl oz/160 ml) Marsala wine
    Salt and freshly ground pepper

1. Prepare the Classic Risotto.
2. If using fresh peas, in a large saucepan of boiling salted
water, blanch the peas until tender, about 8 minutes. Drain.
3. In a large frying pan over medium heat, melt 3 tablespoons of the butter. Add the shallots and sauté, stirring
frequently, until they brown, about 5 minutes.
4. Increase the heat to high. Add the livers and sage and
sauté, stirring frequently, until the livers are brown on the
outside, about 3 minutes. Transfer the livers to a plate.
5. To the frying pan, add the Marsala wine and bring to
a boil, scraping up any browned bits. Boil until syrupy,
about 4 minutes. Add the cooked fresh or thawed peas,
the livers and any juice. Stir until heated through and
glazed, about 1 minute. Add the remaining 2 tablespoons
butter and salt and pepper to taste.
6. To serve, spoon the Classic Risotto onto plates.
Top with the liver mixture.

Serves 6

NUTRITIONAL ANALYSIS: Calories 822 (Kilojoules 3,451); Protein 44 g; Carbohydrates 85 g;
Total Fat 29 g; Saturated Fat 16 g; Cholesterol 557 mg; Sodium 744 mg; Dietary Fiber 4 g

LAMB SHANKS IN WINE WITH CLASSIC RISOTTO

Open your best bottle of full-bodied red wine to pour with this robust winter entrée. As an alternative, serve the braised lamb shanks over Lima Bean Risotto with Pesto (recipe on page 55).

4	tablespoons (2 fl oz/60 ml) olive oil
6	lamb shanks (about 1 lb/ 500 g each)
	Salt and freshly ground pepper
	All-purpose (plain) flour
1	large onion, chopped
3	garlic cloves, peeled and minced
1	large carrot, peeled and chopped
1½	tablespoons tomato paste
2½	cups (20 fl oz/625 ml) dry red wine
2	cups (16 fl oz/500 ml) canned reduced-sodium beef broth
2	bay leaves
3	tablespoons finely chopped fresh marjoram or 2 teaspoons dried
1	recipe Classic Risotto *(recipe on page 10)*
	Fresh marjoram sprigs

1. In a heavy large dutch oven over high heat, heat 2 tablespoons of the olive oil. Season the lamb with salt and pepper to taste, coat with flour and cook until brown, about 4 minutes on each side. Transfer the lamb to a plate.
2. Reduce the heat of the dutch oven to medium. Add the remaining 2 tablespoons olive oil, onion, garlic and carrot and sauté until the onion is translucent, about 8 minutes.
3. Add the tomato paste, wine and broth. Bring to a boil, scraping up any browned bits. Return the lamb to the dutch oven with any juices. Add the bay leaves. Bring to a boil. Reduce the heat, cover and simmer, turning the lamb occasionally, until the lamb is tender, about 1 hour and 45 minutes.
4. Uncover, increase the heat to high and boil until the liquid thickens to sauce consistency, about 15 minutes. Add the chopped marjoram and salt and pepper to taste.
5. Prepare the Classic Risotto.
6. To serve, spoon the Classic Risotto onto a serving plate. Top with the lamb shanks and sauce. Garnish with the marjoram sprigs.

Serves 6

NUTRITIONAL ANALYSIS: Calories 1,122 (Kilojoules 4,711); Protein 66 g; Carbohydrates 86 g; Total Fat 55 g; Saturated Fat 23 g; Cholesterol 185 mg; Sodium 1,032 mg; Dietary Fiber 3 g

 Main Dishes

ROSEMARY-SCENTED TUNA WITH ROSEMARY RISOTTO

Risotto forms an aromatic base for quickly grilled fresh tuna in this impressive yet easy summertime dish. Try grilling some bell peppers (capsicums) and eggplant (aubergines) to serve alongside the fish.

3	tablespoons olive oil
3	tablespoons fresh lemon juice
¼	teaspoon red pepper flakes
3	teaspoons finely chopped fresh rosemary
1½	lb (750 g) tuna steaks
6	cups (48 fl oz/1.5 l) Fish Stock *(recipe on page 127)*
5	tablespoons (3 fl oz/80 ml) olive oil
1	large onion, chopped
2½	cups (17½ oz/545 g) Arborio or medium-grain rice
¾	cup (6 fl oz/180 ml) dry white wine
	Fresh rosemary sprigs

1. In a small glass baking dish, combine the olive oil, lemon juice, red pepper flakes and half of the chopped rosemary. Add the tuna and marinate for 30 minutes.

2. Prepare a fire in an outdoor charcoal grill or preheat a broiler (griller).

3. In a small saucepan over high heat, bring the Fish Stock to a simmer. Reduce the heat to low and keep the liquid hot.

4. In a heavy large saucepan over medium-low heat, heat 2 tablespoons of the olive oil and sauté the onion, stirring frequently, until it is translucent, about 8 minutes.

5. To the onion, add the remaining chopped rosemary and rice and stir until a white spot appears in the center of the grains, about 1 minute. Add the wine and stir until it is absorbed, about 2 minutes. Add ¾ cup (6 fl oz/180 ml) of the stock, adjust the heat to simmer, if needed, so that the liquid bubbles and is absorbed slowly. Stir until the liquid is absorbed. Continue cooking, adding the liquid ¾ cup (6 fl oz/180 ml) at a time and stirring almost constantly, until the rice starts to soften, about 10 minutes. Continue cooking, adding the liquid ½ cup (4 fl oz/125 ml) at a time and stirring almost constantly, until the rice is just tender but slightly firm in the center and the mixture is creamy, about 10 minutes longer. Add the remaining 3 tablespoons olive oil. Stir to mix well.

6. Grill the tuna over a medium-hot fire or broil (grill) until opaque, about 4 minutes per side. Transfer the tuna to a work surface and cube.

7. To serve, spoon the risotto onto plates. Top with the tuna. Garnish with the rosemary sprigs.

Serves 6

NUTRITIONAL ANALYSIS: Calories 634 (Kilojoules 2,663); Protein 30 g; Carbohydrates 72 g; Total Fat 24 g; Saturated Fat 4 g; Cholesterol 39 mg; Sodium 358 mg; Dietary Fiber 2 g

Risotto

LOBSTER, BASIL AND SHALLOT RISOTTO

In this showstopper entrée, risotto gains extraordinary flavor from being cooked in the lobster poaching liquid. The cooking liquid and the lobster can be prepared 6 hours ahead. Cover tightly and refrigerate.

8   cups (64 fl oz/2 l) water

½   onion, cut into large pieces

2   bay leaves

4   fresh parsley sprigs

1   live lobster (about 1½ lb/750 g)

8   tablespoons (4 oz/125 g) unsalted butter

4   shallots, finely chopped

2   cups (14 oz/440 g) Arborio or medium-grain rice

½   cup (4 fl oz/125 ml) dry white wine

1   cup (1½ oz/40 g) finely chopped fresh basil

1½   tablespoons fresh lemon juice

1. In a large dutch oven over high heat, combine the water, onion, bay leaves and parsley and bring to a boil. Add the lobster, cover, reduce the heat to medium and simmer for 12 minutes. Rinse the lobster under cold water. Using a heavy knife, split it down the center. Remove the meat and cube. Return the shells and juices to the cooking liquid and boil to reduce to 5½ cups (44 fl oz/1.4 l), about 10 minutes.

2. Strain the cooking liquid into a small saucepan over high heat and bring to a simmer. Reduce the heat to low and keep the liquid hot.

3. In a heavy large saucepan over medium heat, melt 3 tablespoons of the butter and sauté the shallots, stirring frequently, until they are translucent, about 5 minutes.

4. To the shallots, add the rice and stir until a white spot appears in the center of the grains, about 1 minute. Add the wine and stir until absorbed, about 2 minutes. Add ¾ cup (6 fl oz/180 ml) of the cooking liquid, adjust the heat to simmer, so that the liquid bubbles and is absorbed slowly. Stir until the liquid is absorbed. Continue cooking, adding the liquid ¾ cup (6 fl oz/180 ml) at a time and stirring almost constantly, until the rice starts to soften, about 10 minutes. Continue cooking, adding the liquid ½ cup (4 fl oz/125 ml) at a time and stirring almost constantly, until the rice is just tender but slightly firm in the center and the mixture is creamy, about 10 minutes. Add the lobster meat, basil, lemon juice and remaining 5 tablespoons (2½ oz/75 g) butter. Stir to mix well.

Serves 4

NUTRITIONAL ANALYSIS: Calories 627 (Kilojoules 2,635); Protein 16 g; Carbohydrates 86 g; Total Fat 24 g; Saturated Fat 15 g; Cholesterol 89 mg; Sodium 152 mg; Dietary Fiber 2 g

 Main Dishes

CLAMS WITH FRESH LEMON RISOTTO

*The rice absorbs the juices from the steamed clams, and the lemon zest
further intensifies the flavor of this dish. Because your guests will be
opening their clams at the table, be sure to provide extra napkins.*

Grated zest of 1½ lemons
(see page 126)

6 cups (48 fl oz/1.5 l) Fish Stock
(recipe on page 127) or 3 cups
(24 fl oz/750 ml) bottled clam
juice mixed with 3 cups (24 fl oz/
750 ml) water

3 tablespoons vegetable oil

1 large onion, chopped

2 garlic cloves, peeled and minced

60 small clams (about 4½ lb/2.25 kg),
scrubbed

3 cups (1⅓ lb/655 g) Arborio or
medium-grain rice

¾ cup (6 fl oz/180 ml) dry white wine

3 large Roma (plum) tomatoes,
seeded and chopped *(see page 125)*

½ cup (¾ oz/20 g) chopped flat-leaf
(Italian) parsley
Salt and freshly ground pepper
Fresh flat-leaf (Italian) parsley
sprigs

1. In small saucepan of boiling water, blanch the lemon
zest for 30 seconds. Drain. Repeat, using fresh water.
2. In a small saucepan over high heat, bring the Fish
Stock or clam juice and water to a boil. Reduce the he
to low and keep the liquid hot.
3. In a heavy large dutch oven over medium-low heat,
heat the vegetable oil and sauté the onion and garlic for
5 minutes. Add the clams, discarding any open clams,
cover and cook until the clams open, about 10 minutes.
Using tongs, transfer the clams to a bowl, discarding
any that do not open. Cover and keep warm.
4. To the dutch oven, add the rice and stir over medium
heat until a white spot appears in the center of the grain
about 1 minute. Add the wine and stir until it is absorbe
about 2 minutes. Add the tomatoes and ¾ cup (6 fl oz/
180 ml) of the stock, adjust the heat to simmer, if neede
so that the liquid bubbles and is absorbed slowly. Stir
until the liquid is absorbed. Continue cooking, adding
the liquid ¾ cup (6 fl oz/180 ml) at a time and stirring
almost constantly, until the rice starts to soften, about
10 minutes. Continue cooking, adding the liquid ½ cup
(4 fl oz/125 ml) at a time and stirring almost constantly
until the rice is just tender but slightly firm in the cente
and the mixture is creamy, about 10 minutes longer.
5. Add the lemon zest, chopped parsley and salt and
pepper to taste. Stir to mix well.
6. To serve, spoon into shallow bowls or onto plates.
Top with the clams. Garnish with the parsley sprigs.

Serves 6

NUTRITIONAL ANALYSIS: Calories 501 (Kilojoules 2,103); Protein 15 g; Carbohydrates 90
Total Fat 8 g; Saturated Fat 1 g; Cholesterol 17 mg; Sodium 353 mg; Dietary Fiber 3 g

GARLIC RISOTTO WITH SWORDFISH TOPPING

A fish sauté robust with Sicilian flavors tops a heady risotto. To serve, spoon the risotto onto plates and top with the swordfish mixture. The garlic risotto alone makes a delicious side dish.

5½ cups (44 fl oz/1.4 l) Fish Stock *(recipe on page 127)*

7 tablespoons (4 fl oz/100 ml) olive oil

6 garlic cloves, peeled and thinly sliced

2½ cups (17½ oz/545 g) Arborio or medium-grain rice

1⅔ cups (13 fl oz/410 ml) dry white wine

Salt and freshly ground pepper

1 large onion, chopped

8 large (1½ lb/750 g) Roma (plum) tomatoes, peeled, seeded and chopped *(see page 125)*

1½ lb (750 g) swordfish, cubed

3 tablespoons capers, drained

2 teaspoons dried oregano

1. In a small saucepan over high heat, bring the Fish Stock to a simmer. Reduce the heat to low and keep the liquid hot.
2. In a heavy large saucepan over medium heat, heat 2 tablespoons of the olive oil and sauté the garlic, stirring frequently, until it begins to color, about 4 minutes.
3. To the garlic, add the rice and stir until a white spot appears in the center of the grains, about 1 minute. Add ⅔ cup (5 fl oz/160 ml) of the wine and stir until absorbed, about 2 minutes. Add ¾ cup (6 fl oz/180 ml) of the stock, adjust the heat to simmer, if needed, so that the liquid bubbles and is absorbed slowly. Stir until the liquid is absorbed. Continue cooking, adding the liquid ¾ cup (6 fl oz/180 ml) at a time and stirring almost constantly, until the rice starts to soften, about 10 minutes. Continue cooking, adding the liquid ½ cup (4 fl oz/125 ml) at a time and stirring almost constantly, until the rice is just tender but slightly firm in the center and the mixture is creamy, about 10 minutes longer. Add 2 tablespoons of the olive oil and salt and pepper to taste.
4. In a heavy large frying pan over medium heat, heat the remaining 3 tablespoons olive oil and sauté the onion, stirring frequently, until it is translucent, about 8 minutes. Add the tomatoes and simmer until soft, about 5 minutes.
5. Add the swordfish and stir until it is opaque on the outside, about 2 minutes. Add the remaining 1 cup (8 fl oz/250 ml) wine. Increase the heat to high and boil, stirring frequently, until the fish is opaque throughout, about 3 minutes. Add the capers and oregano.

Serves 6

NUTRITIONAL ANALYSIS: Calories 655 (Kilojoules 2,753); Protein 30 g; Carbohydrates 78 g; Total Fat 21 g; Saturated Fat 4 g; Cholesterol 44 mg; Sodium 516 mg; Dietary Fiber 4 g

Main Dishes

PORCINI MUSHROOM AND SPICY SAUSAGE RISOTTO

If you prefer a more mild meal, substitute sweet Italian sausage for the spicy, hot variety as the porcini mushrooms provide plenty of flavor. Garnish with a sprig of fresh rosemary.

1½ oz (45 g) dried porcini mushrooms

3 cups (24 fl oz/750 ml) hot water

2½ cups (20 fl oz/625 ml) Chicken Stock *(recipe on page 127)*

1 tablespoon olive oil

1 large onion, chopped

8 oz (250 g) fresh hot Italian sausages, casings removed

12 oz (375 g) button mushrooms, sliced

1½ teaspoons finely chopped fresh rosemary or ½ teaspoon dried

2½ cups (17½ oz/545 g) Arborio or medium-grain rice

¾ cup (6 fl oz/180 ml) dry white wine

1 bay leaf

⅓ cup (3 fl oz/80 ml) half & half (half cream)

2 cups (8 oz/250 g) freshly grated Parmesan cheese

Salt and freshly ground pepper

1. In a small bowl, soak the porcini mushrooms in the hot water until soft, about 20 minutes. Drain, reserving the soaking liquid. Chop the porcini mushrooms.

2. In a small saucepan over high heat, combine the Chicken Stock and mushroom soaking liquid and bring to a simmer. Reduce the heat to low and keep the liquid hot.

3. In a heavy large saucepan over medium heat, heat the olive oil and sauté the onion, stirring frequently, until it begins to soften, about 5 minutes. Add the sausage meat, increase the heat to high and cook, breaking up the meat with a fork, just until it is no longer pink, about 6 minutes. Add the button mushrooms and chopped rosemary and stir until the mushrooms begin to soften, about 5 minutes.

4. To the sausage mixture, add the porcini mushrooms and the rice and stir for 1 minute. Add the wine and bay leaf and stir until the wine is absorbed, about 2 minutes. Add ¾ cup (6 fl oz/180 ml) of the stock, adjust the heat to simmer, if needed, so that the liquid bubbles and is absorbed slowly. Stir until the liquid is absorbed. Continue cooking, adding the liquid ¾ cup (6 fl oz/180 ml) at a time and stirring almost constantly, until the rice starts to soften, about 10 minutes. Continue cooking, adding the liquid ½ cup (4 fl oz/125 ml) at a time and stirring almost constantly, until the rice is just tender but slightly firm in the center and the mixture is creamy, about 10 minutes longer.

5. Mix in the half & half, Parmesan cheese and salt and pepper to taste. Remove and discard the bay leaf.

Serves 6

NUTRITIONAL ANALYSIS: Calories 675 (Kilojoules 2,835); Protein 28 g; Carbohydrates 79 g; Total Fat 27 g; Saturated Fat 12 g; Cholesterol 59 mg; Sodium 944 mg; Dietary Fiber 3 g

SHRIMP AND BROCCOLI WITH SAFFRON RISOTTO

Saffron infuses this risotto with an intense aroma and flavor. Try substituting scallops for the shrimp, and snowpeas (mangetout) for the broccoli. If saffron is unavailable, use a few tablespoons of minced fresh parsley instead.

6 cups (48 fl oz/1.5 l) Fish Stock *(recipe on page 127)*

4 cups (12 oz/375 g) broccoli florets

1 teaspoon saffron threads

4 tablespoons (2 oz/60 g) unsalted butter

2 garlic cloves, peeled and crushed

1 onion, chopped

3 cups (1⅓ lb/655 g) Arborio or medium-grain rice

¾ cup (6 fl oz/180 ml) dry white wine

1½ lb (750 g) medium shrimp (prawns), peeled and deveined *(see page 125)*

4 Roma (plum) tomatoes, seeded and chopped *(see page 125)*

Salt and freshly ground pepper

1. In a small saucepan over high heat, bring the Fish Stock to a boil. Add the broccoli and boil until it begins to soften, about 3 minutes. Using a slotted spoon, transfer the broccoli to a small bowl. Add the saffron to the stock. Reduce the heat to low and keep the liquid hot.

2. In a heavy large saucepan over low heat, melt 2 tablespoons of the butter and cook the garlic, stirring frequently, until it is golden brown, about 2 minutes. Discard the garlic. Add the onion and sauté until it is tender, stirring frequently, about 8 minutes.

3. To the onion, add the rice and stir until a white spot appears in the center of the grains, about 1 minute. Add the wine and stir until it is absorbed, about 2 minutes. Add ¾ cup (6 fl oz/180 ml) of the stock, adjust the heat to simmer, if needed, so that the liquid bubbles and is absorbed slowly. Stir until the liquid is absorbed. Continue cooking, adding the liquid ¾ cup (6 fl oz/180 ml) at a time and stirring almost constantly, until the rice starts to soften, about 10 minutes. Reserve ½ cup (4 fl oz/125 ml) of the liquid for step 4. Continue cooking, adding the liquid ½ cup (4 fl oz/125 ml) at a time and stirring almost constantly for 6 minutes longer.

4. Add the shrimp and tomatoes and continue cooking, stirring frequently and adding the reserved liquid, ¼ cup (2 fl oz/60 ml) at a time, until the shrimp are pink, the rice is tender and the mixture is creamy, about 4 minutes.

5. Add the broccoli, the remaining 2 tablespoons butter and salt and pepper to taste. Stir to mix well.

Serves 6

NUTRITIONAL ANALYSIS: Calories 581 (Kilojoules 2,439); Protein 29 g; Carbohydrates 91 g; Total Fat 10 g; Saturated Fat 5 g; Cholesterol 161 mg; Sodium 473 mg; Dietary Fiber 5 g

Main Dishes

$\mathscr{H}$AM, PEA AND PARMESAN RISOTTO

A variation on the classic pasta dish fettuccine Alfredo, this creamy risotto is especially satisfying on a cold winter's night. For a vegetarian version, leave out the ham and substitute Vegetable Stock for the Chicken Stock.

6 cups (48 fl oz/1.5 l) Chicken Stock *(recipe on page 127)*

2 tablespoons unsalted butter

1 onion, chopped

12 oz (375 g) ham, cut into ½-inch (12-mm) pieces

2½ cups (17½ oz/545 g) Arborio or medium-grain rice

2 cups (10 oz/315 g) shelled fresh peas *(see page 124)* or frozen peas

1 cup (4 oz/125 g) freshly grated Parmesan cheese

1 tablespoon finely chopped fresh thyme or 1 teaspoon dried

Salt and freshly ground pepper

Fresh thyme sprigs

1. In a small saucepan over high heat, bring the Chicken Stock to a simmer. Reduce the heat to low and keep the liquid hot.

2. In a heavy large saucepan over medium-low heat, melt the butter and sauté the onion stirring frequently, for 5 minutes. Add the ham and cook until the onion is tender, stirring frequently, about 5 minutes longer.

3. To the onion mixture, add the rice and stir until a white spot appears in the center of the grains, about 1 minute. Add ¾ cup (6 fl oz/180 ml) of the stock, adjust the heat to simmer, if needed, so that the liquid bubbles and is absorbed slowly. Stir until the liquid is absorbed. Continue cooking, adding the liquid ¾ cup (6 fl oz/180 ml) at a time and stirring almost constantly, until the rice starts to soften, about 10 minutes.

4. Add the peas and continue cooking, adding the liquid ½ cup (4 fl oz/125 ml) at a time and stirring almost constantly, until the rice is just tender but slightly firm in the center and the mixture is creamy, about 10 minutes longer.

5. Add the Parmesan cheese, chopped thyme and salt and pepper to taste. Stir to mix well.

6. To serve, spoon into bowls or onto plates. Garnish with the thyme sprigs.

Serves 6

NUTRITIONAL ANALYSIS: Calories 584 (Kilojoules 2,454); Protein 28 g; Carbohydrates 79 g; Total Fat 18 g; Saturated Fat 8 g; Cholesterol 56 mg; Sodium 1,169 mg; Dietary Fiber 4 g

Other Rice Dishes

MOROCCAN-FLAVORED RICE AND CHICKEN SALAD

Turmeric, ginger, cumin, cinnamon and cayenne combine to give this unique rice salad the intriguing tastes and aromas of North African cuisine. Packaged honey-roasted almonds can be substituted for the toasted nuts.

3   large chicken breast halves, about 2¼ lb (1.1 kg) total weight

     Salt and freshly ground pepper

1   large red (Spanish) onion, diced

1   large red bell pepper (capsicum), stemmed, seeded, deribbed and cut into ¾-inch (2-cm) cubes *(see page 124)*

2   zucchini (courgettes), cut into ¾-inch (2-cm) cubes

9   tablespoons (4½ fl oz/135 ml) olive oil

½   teaspoon ground cinnamon

½   teaspoon ground cumin

½   teaspoon ground ginger

½   teaspoon ground turmeric

1½   cups (10½ oz/330 g) long-grain rice

2¾   cups (22 fl oz/675 ml) water

15½   oz (485 g) canned chick-peas (garbanzo beans), drained

½   cup (⅔ oz/20 g) finely chopped fresh parsley

3   tablespoons fresh lemon juice

⅛   teaspoon cayenne pepper

¾   cup (4 oz/125 g) almonds, toasted and coarsely chopped *(see page 123)*

     Fresh flat-leaf (Italian) parsley sprigs

1. Preheat an oven to 450°F (230°C).

2. In a small roasting pan, place the chicken. Season with the salt and pepper to taste. Roast the chicken until just cooked through, about 30 minutes. Cool the chicken. Skin the chicken, remove the meat from the bones and cut into ½-inch (12-mm) cubes.

3. In a large roasting pan, arrange the onion, bell pepper and zucchini. Add 2 tablespoons of the olive oil. Sprinkle with salt and pepper to taste. Toss to coat the vegetables. Roast the vegetables until tender, stirring occasionally, about 25 minutes.

4. In a heavy medium saucepan over high heat, heat 1 tablespoon of the olive oil. Add the cinnamon, cumin, ginger, turmeric and rice. Stir until the mixture is aromatic, about 2 minutes. Add the water and bring to a boil. Reduce the heat to low, cover and cook until the water is absorbed, about 20 minutes.

5. In a large bowl, combine the rice, chicken, roasted vegetables, garbanzo beans and parsley.

6. In a small bowl, place the lemon juice. Gradually mix in the remaining 6 tablespoons (3 fl oz/90 ml) olive oil. Add the cayenne. Add to the rice mixture. Toss to mix well. Cover and refrigerate for up to 6 hours.

7. To serve, transfer to a serving bowl. Sprinkle with the almonds. Garnish with the parsley sprigs.

Serves 6

NUTRITIONAL ANALYSIS: Calories 764 (Kilojoules 3,210); Protein 50 g; Carbohydrates 61 g; Total Fat 36 g; Saturated Fat 5 g; Cholesterol 104 mg; Sodium 186 mg; Dietary Fiber 6 g

ROSEMARY AND WALNUT HERB CROQUETTES

*Just as tasty and satisfying as supplì, these croquettes are a little easier
to form. The recipe can be varied in many ways. Replace the rosemary with
another herb or substitute pine nuts for the walnuts.*

2 cups (16 fl oz/500 ml) Chicken or Vegetable Stock *(recipes on pages 126–127)*

1 cup (7 oz/220 g) Arborio rice or medium-grain rice

⅓ cup (1 oz/30 g) freshly grated Parmesan cheese

1½ teaspoons finely chopped fresh rosemary or ½ teaspoon dried

⅓ cup (1 oz/30 g) chopped walnuts

Salt and freshly ground pepper

1 egg, lightly beaten

½ cup (2 oz/60 g) dried bread crumbs *(see page 122)*

Vegetable oil or olive oil for frying

Fresh rosemary sprigs

1. In a medium saucepan over high heat, bring the Chicken or Vegetable Stock to a boil. Add the rice and bring to a boil, stirring occasionally. Reduce the heat to low, cover and cook until the liquid is absorbed, about 20 minutes. Remove from the heat.

2. Add the Parmesan cheese, chopped rosemary, walnuts and salt and pepper to taste. Mix in the egg. Refrigerate until firm enough to shape, about 2 hours.

3. To make the croquettes, line a baking sheet with waxed paper. Place the bread crumbs in a cake pan. Form the rice mixture into 18 1½-inch (4-cm) balls. Roll them in the bread crumbs to coat. Transfer to the baking sheet. Cover and refrigerate for at least 1 hour or up to 24 hours.

4. Preheat an oven to 250°F (120°C).

5. In a heavy large frying pan over medium-high heat, heat enough oil to coat the bottom of the pan. Working in batches, add the croquettes and, using a spatula, flatten each to a ½-inch (12-mm) thickness. Fry until golden brown, about 2 minutes on each side. Using a spatula, remove the croquettes and drain on paper towels. Transfer to a baking sheet and keep warm in the oven while cooking the remaining croquettes.

6. To serve, transfer the croquettes to a platter. Garnish with the rosemary sprigs.

Serves 6

NUTRITIONAL ANALYSIS: Calories 287 (Kilojoules 1,204); Protein 8 g; Carbohydrates 35 g; Total Fat 13 g; Saturated Fat 3 g; Cholesterol 39 mg; Sodium 207 mg; Dietary Fiber 1 g

Other Rice Dishes

$\mathcal{S}$PANISH PAELLA WITH SEAFOOD

Spain's national challenger to risotto makes a wonderful main course for a dinner party, especially when paired with ice-cold pitchers of the red-wine and fruit punch known as sangría.

10 cups (2½ qt/2.5 l) Fish Stock *(recipe on page 127)*

1 cup (5 oz/155 g) shelled fresh peas *(see page 124)* or frozen peas, thawed

½ cup (4 fl oz/125 ml) dry white wine

1 teaspoon saffron threads

¼ cup (2 fl oz/60 ml) olive oil

1 large onion, chopped

1 large red bell pepper (capsicum), stemmed, seeded, deribbed and cut into ¾-inch (2-cm) pieces *(see page 124)*

4 large garlic cloves, peeled and finely chopped

8 oz (250 g) chorizo or hot Italian sausage, casings removed

2 teaspoons paprika
Red pepper flakes

4 Roma (plum) tomatoes, peeled, seeded and chopped *(see page 125)*

3 cups (1⅓ lb/655 g) Arborio or medium-grain rice

1¼ lb (625 g) medium shrimp (prawns), peeled and deveined *(see page 125)*

24 mussels (about 2 lb/1 kg), scrubbed and debearded

1. In a medium saucepan over high heat, bring the Fish Stock to a boil. Add the fresh peas, if using, and cook until tender, about 8 minutes. Using a slotted spoon, remove the peas and reserve.

2. Reduce the heat to medium and simmer until the liquid is reduced to 5½ cups (44 fl oz/1.4 l), about 15 minutes. Add the wine and saffron and bring to a simmer. Reduce the heat to low and keep the liquid hot.

3. In a paella pan or heavy large dutch oven over medium heat, heat the oil and sauté the onion, stirring frequently, until it begins to soften, about 3 minutes. Add the bell pepper and cook until it begins to soften, about 3 minutes. Add the garlic and sausage and cook, breaking the sausage up with a fork, until it is no longer pink, about 5 minutes. Add the paprika and red pepper flakes to taste and stir until the mixture is aromatic, about 30 seconds. Add the tomatoes.

4. Add the rice and stir until a white spot appears in the center of the grains, about 1 minute. Add the stock mixture. Increase the heat to high and bring the mixture to a boil, stirring constantly. Reduce the heat to low, cover and simmer for 15 minutes, stirring occasionally.

5. Add the shrimp, cooked or thawed peas and mussels, discarding any open mussels. Cover and cook until the shrimp are just pink, the mussels open and the liquid is absorbed, about 10 minutes longer. Remove from the heat and let stand, covered, for 10 minutes. Discard any mussels that do not open.

Serves 6

NUTRITIONAL ANALYSIS: Calories 795 (Kilojoules 3,337); Protein 36 g; Carbohydrates 98 g; Total Fat 28 g; Saturated Fat 7 g; Cholesterol 154 mg; Sodium 1,026 mg; Dietary Fiber 5 g

SUPPLÌ WITH CHEESE AND PORCINI MUSHROOMS

This traditional Italian preparation is a great way to transform leftover risotto into a fanciful side dish to pair with a salad. Step-by-step photographs of how to make supplì are on page 15.

1 oz (30 g) dried porcini
   mushrooms

2 cups (16 fl oz/500 ml) hot water

2 cups (10 oz/315 g) Classic Risotto
   (recipe on page 10)

2 eggs, lightly beaten

¾ cup (3 oz/90 g) dried bread crumbs
   (see page 122)

3 oz (90 g) Fontina, Gouda or
   mozzarella cheese, cut into
   12 strips

   Vegetable oil for deep-frying

1. In a small bowl, combine the porcini mushrooms and hot water. Let stand until the mushrooms soften, about 30 minutes. Drain the mushrooms, reserving the soaking liquid. Chop the mushrooms and place in a small saucepan over medium-high heat. Add the soaking liquid (discarding any sediment in the bottom of the bowl). Boil until all the liquid evaporates, about 8 minutes. Remove from the heat.
2. In a medium bowl, combine the Classic Risotto and eggs.
3. To make the supplì, line a baking sheet with waxed paper. Place the bread crumbs in a cake pan. Drop 1 tablespoon of the risotto mixture on to the bread crumbs. Place 1 cheese strip and 1 teaspoon of the porcini mixture in the center of the risotto mound. Top with 1 tablespoon of the risotto mixture. Using your hands, gently form the risotto, cheese and porcini into a cylinder. Roll in the bread crumbs to coat. Transfer to the baking sheet. Repeat to make 12 supplì. Cover and refrigerate for at least 1 hour and up to 24 hours.
4. Preheat an oven to 250°F (120°C).
5. To a large saucepan, add oil to a depth of 2 inches (5 cm). Heat to 350°F (180°C). Working in batches, fry the supplì, turning occasionally, until golden brown, about 3 minutes. Drain on paper towels. Transfer to a baking sheet and keep warm in the oven while cooking the remaining supplì.
6. To serve, transfer to individual plates.

Serves 6

NUTRITIONAL ANALYSIS: Calories 361 (Kilojoules 1,518); Protein 15 g; Carbohydrates 38 g; Total Fat 17 g; Saturated Fat 7 g; Cholesterol 98 mg; Sodium 475 mg; Dietary Fiber 1 g

$\mathscr{A}$RROZ CON POLLO

Translated as "rice with chicken," this specialty of Valencia, Spain, is simply a paella without seafood. If you like, you can make the dish even easier to serve and eat by using boneless and skinless pieces of chicken.

3½ cups (28 fl oz/875 ml) Chicken Stock *(recipe on page 127)*

2 tablespoons olive oil

3¼ lb (1.6 kg) chicken, cut into 8 pieces
Salt and freshly ground pepper

1 large onion, chopped

1 *each* large red and green bell pepper (capsicum), stemmed, seeded, deribbed and cut into strips *(see page 124)*

3 garlic cloves, peeled and minced

1 tablespoon paprika
Red pepper flakes

2 large tomatoes, seeded and chopped *(see page 125)*

¼ teaspoon saffron threads

2 cups (14 oz/440 g) medium-grain or long-grain rice

½ cup (4 fl oz/125 ml) dry white wine
Salt

¼ cup chopped fresh parsley

1. In a small saucepan over high heat, bring the Chicken Stock to a simmer. Reduce the heat to low and keep the liquid hot.

2. In a heavy large dutch oven over medium-high heat, heat the olive oil. Season the chicken with salt and pepper to taste. Place in the dutch oven and cook until brown, 5 minutes on each side. Transfer the chicken to a plate.

3. Pour off all but a thin film of oil from the dutch oven and set the dutch oven over medium heat. Add the onion, bell peppers and garlic and sauté, stirring frequently, until the onion is translucent, about 8 minutes. Add the paprika and red pepper flakes to taste and sauté for 30 seconds. Add the tomatoes and saffron. Cook, stirring frequently, until most of the liquid evaporates, about 5 minutes.

4. Add the rice and stir until a white spot appears in the center of the grains, about 1 minute. Add the stock and wine and salt to taste. Bring to a boil. Add the chicken and any juices on the plate. Return to a boil.

5. Reduce the heat to low, cover and cook until the rice is tender and the chicken is opaque throughout, about 30 minutes. Remove from the heat and let stand, covered, for 5 minutes.

6. To serve, transfer to individual plates. Garnish with the parsley.

Serves 6

NUTRITIONAL ANALYSIS: Calories 631 (Kilojoules 2,652); Protein 37 g; Carbohydrates 63 g; Total Fat 26 g; Saturated Fat 7 g; Cholesterol 99 mg; Sodium 532 mg; Dietary Fiber 3 g

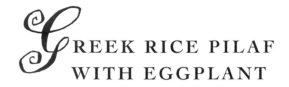

GREEK RICE PILAF WITH EGGPLANT

This typically Greek combination makes a delicious side dish for roast lamb or chicken or grilled seafood. Try substituting some fresh mint for the dill. For a richer effect, add crumbled feta cheese along with the butter and herbs.

1 large globe eggplant (aubergine), trimmed, cut into ³⁄₄-inch (2-cm) cubes

1½ teaspoons salt

5 tablespoons (3 fl oz/80 ml) olive oil

1 large onion, chopped

2 zucchini (courgettes), cut into ³⁄₄-inch (2-cm) cubes

2 cups (14 oz/440 g) long-grain rice

3¼ cups (26 fl oz/800 ml) Vegetable or Chicken Stock *(recipes on pages 126–127)*

¼ cup (2 fl oz/60 ml) fresh lemon juice

1 tablespoon unsalted butter

3 tablespoons finely chopped fresh flat-leaf (Italian) parsley

3 tablespoons finely chopped fresh dill

Salt and freshly ground pepper

³⁄₄ cup (4 oz/125 g) almonds, toasted and coarsely chopped *(see page 123)*

1. In a large colander, mix the eggplant and the 1½ teaspoons salt. Let stand for 30 minutes.

2. Pat the eggplant dry with paper towels. In a heavy large frying pan over medium-high heat, heat 3 tablespoons of the olive oil and cook the eggplant, stirring frequently, until it begins to soften, about 6 minutes. Remove from the heat.

3. In a heavy large saucepan over medium heat, heat the remaining 2 tablespoons olive oil and sauté the onion, stirring frequently, until translucent, about 5 minutes. Add the zucchini and sauté for 3 minutes. Add the rice and stir for 2 minutes. Add the Vegetable or Chicken Stock and lemon juice. Increase the heat to high and bring to a boil. Reduce the heat to low, cover and cook for 10 minutes. Add the eggplant, cover and cook until the liquid is absorbed, about 10 minutes longer.

4. Remove from the heat. Add the butter, parsley, dill and salt and pepper to taste.

5. To serve, transfer to individual plates. Sprinkle with the almonds.

Serves 6

NUTRITIONAL ANALYSIS: Calories 535 (Kilojoules 2,248); Protein 11 g; Carbohydrates 72 g; Total Fat 24 g; Saturated Fat 4 g; Cholesterol 5 mg; Sodium 204 mg; Dietary Fiber 6 g

RICE MINESTRONE

Minestrone is traditionally made with pasta, but a generous quantity of white rice makes this version a satisfying alternative. Enjoy the soup as a first course or light meal.

2   tablespoons olive oil
3   cups (9 oz/280 g) thinly sliced cabbage
2   zucchini (courgettes), diced
1   large carrot, peeled and diced
1   large onion, chopped
6   cups (48 fl oz/1.5 l) Chicken or Vegetable Stock
    (recipes on pages 126–127)
1   cup (7 oz/220 g) long-grain rice
15 oz (470 g) canned cannellini (white kidney beans)
    or Great Northern beans, rinsed and drained
⅓ cup (½ oz/15 g) sliced fresh basil
    Salt and freshly ground pepper

1. In a heavy large saucepan over medium-high heat, heat the olive oil. Add the cabbage, zucchini, carrot and onion. Cook until the vegetables are soft, stirring frequently, about 10 minutes.
2. Add the Chicken or Vegetable Stock and rice and bring to a boil. Reduce the heat and simmer for 10 minutes, stirring occasionally.
3. Add the beans and simmer, stirring occasionally, until the rice is tender, about 10 minutes. Add the basil and salt and pepper to taste. Stir to mix well.
4. To serve, ladle into individual bowls.

Serves 6

NUTRITIONAL ANALYSIS: Calories 278 (Kilojoules 1,169); Protein 11 g; Carbohydrates 46 g; Total Fat 8 g; Saturated Fat 1 g; Cholesterol 0 mg; Sodium 222 mg; Dietary Fiber 6 g

GRAPE LEAVES STUFFED WITH RICE AND PINE NUTS

Virtually every taverna in Greece offers up this savory-sweet appetizer of rice wrapped in brine-packed grape leaves. Vary the flavor of the filling, if you like, by replacing the mint with dill and parsley.

¼ cup (2 fl oz/60 ml) plus 1 tablespoon olive oil

2 large onions, chopped

1 teaspoon ground allspice

2 cups (14 oz/440 g) long-grain rice

⅔ cup (4 oz/125 g) dried currants

½ cup (¾ oz/20 g) finely chopped fresh mint

5¼ cups (42 fl oz/1.3 l) hot water or as needed

Salt and freshly ground pepper

½ cup (2½ oz/75 g) pine nuts

8 oz (250 g) bottled grape leaves, rinsed, drained and tough stems trimmed

1. In a heavy large saucepan over medium-high heat, heat the ¼ cup (2 fl oz/60 ml) olive oil and sauté the onions, stirring frequently, until they are translucent, about 8 minutes.
2. Add the allspice and rice and stir for 1 minute. Add the currants, mint and 1¼ cups (10 fl oz/300 ml) of the hot water. Reduce the heat to low, cover and simmer, stirring occasionally, until the rice is partially cooked and no liquid remains, about 12 minutes. Remove from the heat. Add salt and pepper to taste.
3. In a heavy small frying pan over medium-low heat, heat the 1 tablespoon olive oil. Add the pine nuts and stir until golden brown, about 3 minutes. Add to the rice.
4. In a large wide saucepan, place enough grape leaves to cover the bottom. Place 1 grape leaf, vein-side up, on a work surface. Spoon 2 tablespoons of the rice mixture onto the center of the widest part of the leaf. Fold the bottom of the leaf over the filling. Fold the sides in, then roll the leaf up to enclose the rice. Place, seam-side down, over the grape leaves in the saucepan. Repeat to make 36.
5. Pour enough hot water into the saucepan to just cover the grape leaves. Place a heatproof plate over the leaves. Cover the saucepan.
6. Simmer over medium-low heat until the leaves are tender and the rice is cooked through, about 45 minutes.
7. To serve, using tongs, transfer the stuffed leaves to a platter. Cool to room temperature.

Serves 6

NUTRITIONAL ANALYSIS: Calories 516 (Kilojoules 2,169); Protein 9 g; Carbohydrates 76 g; Total Fat 18 g; Saturated Fat 3 g; Cholesterol 0 mg; Sodium 1,208 mg; Dietary Fiber 4 g

Other Rice Dishes

RICE, ARUGULA, ASPARAGUS AND GREEN BEAN SALAD

Rice often gets overlooked as a main ingredient for salads. In this spring or summer side dish, it perfectly highlights crisp vegetables. Serve on a bed of mixed salad greens.

2¾ cups (22 fl oz/675 ml) water
1½ cups (10½ oz/330 g) long-grain rice
1 lb (500 g) asparagus, cut into 1-inch (2.5-cm) pieces
8 oz (250 g) green beans, cut into 1-inch (2.5-cm) pieces
1 tablespoon plus 1 teaspoon Dijon-style mustard
2 tablespoons plus 2 teaspoons white wine vinegar
½ cup (4 fl oz/125 ml) olive oil
1 cup (1 oz/30 g) lightly packed arugula, chopped
3 green (spring) onions, green and white parts, chopped
Salt and freshly ground pepper

1. In a medium saucepan over high heat, bring the water to a boil. Add the rice. Return to a boil. Reduce the heat to low, cover and cook until the water is absorbed, about 20 minutes. Fluff the rice with a fork, transfer to a large bowl and cool.
2. In a large saucepan of boiling salted water, cook the asparagus and green beans until just tender-crisp, about 5 minutes. Drain and rinse with cold water.
3. To make the dressing, in a small bowl, mix the mustard and vinegar until smooth. Gradually mix in the olive oil.
4. To the rice, add the asparagus, beans, arugula and green onions. Gently mix in the dressing. Add salt and pepper to taste. Refrigerate until well chilled, at least 1 hour.
5. To serve, transfer to individual plates.

Serves 6

NUTRITIONAL ANALYSIS: Calories 376 (Kilojoules 1,578); Protein 7 g; Carbohydrates 46 g; Total Fat 19 g; Saturated Fat 3 g; Cholesterol 0 mg; Sodium 89 mg; Dietary Fiber 2 g

TOMATO AND TARRAGON RICE SOUP

An old favorite soup here gains a somewhat more sophisticated character by the addition of anise-flavored fennel bulb and seeds. The tarragon may be replaced, if you like, with fresh basil.

4   bacon slices, chopped

1   large onion, chopped

1   fennel bulb, thinly sliced crosswise

1   red bell pepper (capsicum), stemmed, seeded, deribbed and chopped *(see page 124)*

1   teaspoon fennel seeds, crushed

½   cup (3½ oz/105 g) long-grain rice

3½ cups (28 fl oz/875 ml) Chicken or Vegetable Stock *(recipes on pages 126–127)*

5   large tomatoes, peeled, seeded and chopped *(see page 125)*

8   oz (250 g) canned tomato sauce

2   tablespoons finely chopped fresh tarragon or 1½ teaspoons dried

Salt and freshly ground pepper

Fresh tarragon sprigs

1. In a heavy large saucepan over medium heat, cook the bacon, stirring frequently, until it is almost crisp, about 3 minutes. Add the onion, fennel bulb, bell pepper and fennel seeds and sauté, stirring frequently, until the onion is translucent, about 8 minutes.

2. Add the rice, Chicken or Vegetable Stock, tomatoes with their juice and tomato sauce and bring to a boil. Reduce the heat and simmer, stirring occasionally, until the rice is tender, about 25 minutes.

3. Add the chopped tarragon and salt and pepper to taste. Stir to mix well.

4. To serve, ladle into individual bowls. Garnish with the tarragon sprigs.

Serves 6

NUTRITIONAL ANALYSIS: Calories 223 (Kilojoules 935); Protein 7 g; Carbohydrates 28 g; Total Fat 11 g; Saturated Fat 4 g; Cholesterol 10 mg; Sodium 448 mg; Dietary Fiber 4 g

$\mathscr{R}$ICE CUSTARD PUDDING

As good as it already is, this pudding will become even more luxurious if you replace a third of the milk with an equal amount of heavy (double) cream. For an especially festive touch, team the dessert with mixed berries.

¾ cup (4½ oz/140 g) raisins

3 tablespoons brandy

1 cup (8 fl oz/250 ml) water

½ cup (3½ oz/105 g) long-grain rice

3 cups (24 fl oz/750 ml) milk

¾ cup (6 oz/185 g) sugar

1½ teaspoons vanilla extract (essence)

½ teaspoon grated lemon zest
    (see page 126)

½ teaspoon grated orange zest
    (see page 126)

4 eggs, lightly beaten
    Strips of zest from 1 lemon
    (see page 126)

    Strips of zest from 1 orange
    (see page 126)

1. Preheat an oven to 300°F (150°C). Butter an 8-inch (20-cm) square glass baking dish or any shallow 2-qt (2-l) baking dish.

2. In a small bowl, combine the raisins and brandy. Soak while cooking the rice.

3. In a small saucepan, bring the water to a boil. Stir in the rice. Reduce the heat to low, cover and cook until the water is absorbed, about 20 minutes.

4. Remove the rice from the heat. Mix in the milk, sugar, vanilla and grated lemon and orange zests. Drain the raisins and add. Mix in the eggs. Transfer the mixture to the prepared baking dish.

5. Place the baking dish in a large baking pan. Pour enough hot water into the baking pan to come halfway up the sides of the baking dish. Place in the oven and bake until a knife inserted near the edge of the pudding comes out clean, about 1 hour (the center will still be soft). Remove from the oven. Cool the custard slightly or refrigerate until well chilled, up to 2 days.

6. To serve, spoon into bowls. Garnish with the strips of lemon and orange zests.

Serves 6

NUTRITIONAL ANALYSIS: Calories 368 (Kilojoules 1,544); Protein 10 g; Carbohydrates 65 g; Total Fat 8 g; Saturated Fat 4 g; Cholesterol 160 mg; Sodium 112 mg; Dietary Fiber 1 g

OLD-FASHIONED RICE PUDDING WITH RAISINS

Simple and undeniably delicious, this classic can be enjoyed either warm or cold. Maple syrup adds an especially comforting nuance, but you could substitute an equal amount of dark brown sugar.

3⅓ cups (27 fl oz/825 ml) milk or more as needed

⅔ cup (5 oz/155 g) Arborio or medium-grain rice

½ cup (3 oz/90 g) golden raisins (sultanas)

½ cup (4 oz/125 g) sugar

¼ teaspoon salt

3 tablespoons pure maple syrup

1 teaspoon vanilla extract (essence)

Grated nutmeg

1. In a heavy medium saucepan over high heat, combine the milk, rice, raisins, sugar and salt. Bring to a boil, stirring occasionally. Reduce the heat to low and cook, uncovered, stirring frequently, until the rice is tender and the mixture is thick, about 40 minutes.

2. Add the maple syrup, vanilla and nutmeg to taste. Stir to mix well.

3. To serve, spoon the hot pudding into bowls. Or, refrigerate the pudding for up to 2 days and thin with the additional milk, if needed, before serving cold.

Serves 6

NUTRITIONAL ANALYSIS: Calories 312 (Kilojoules 1,312); Protein 6 g; Carbohydrates 62 g; Total Fat 5 g; Saturated Fat 3 g; Cholesterol 19 mg; Sodium 159 mg; Dietary Fiber 1 g

RICE PUDDING WITH DATES, HONEY AND PISTACHIOS

This version of rice pudding gains intrigue from the inclusion of exotic ingredients from Moroccan cuisine. Try other dried fruit such as apricots or figs, if you like, in place of the dates, and almonds instead of the pistachios.

3½ cups (28 fl oz/875 ml) milk or more as needed

⅔ cup (5 oz/155 g) Arborio or medium-grain rice

¼ cup (2 oz/60 g) sugar

¼ cup (3 oz/90 g) plus 2 tablespoons honey

2 teaspoons grated orange zest *(see page 126)*

¼ teaspoon salt

½ cup (2½ oz/75 g) pitted and chopped dates

1 teaspoon vanilla extract (essence)

¼ teaspoon ground cinnamon

⅓ cup (1 oz/30 g) unsalted roasted pistachio nuts, chopped

Strips of zest from 1 lemon *(see page 126)*

1. In a heavy medium saucepan over medium heat, combine the milk, rice, sugar, the ¼ cup (3 oz/90 g) honey, the orange zest and salt. Bring to a simmer, stirring until the sugar dissolves. Reduce the heat to low and cook, uncovered, stirring frequently, until the pudding is thick and the rice is tender, about 40 minutes.

2. Add the dates and cook, stirring frequently, for 5 minutes. Add the vanilla, cinnamon and the 2 tablespoons honey. Stir to mix well.

3. Thin with the additional milk, if needed. Cover and refrigerate until well chilled, up to 2 days.

4. To serve, spoon the pudding into bowls. Sprinkle with the pistachios. Garnish with the lemon zest.

Serves 6

NUTRITIONAL ANALYSIS: Calories 337 (Kilojoules 1,417); Protein 7 g; Carbohydrates 63 g; Total Fat 7 g; Saturated Fat 3 g; Cholesterol 20 mg; Sodium 162 mg; Dietary Fiber 1 g

BASIC TERMS AND TECHNIQUES

The following entries provide a reference source for this volume, offering definitions of essential or unusual ingredients and explanations of fundamental techniques as they relate to the preparation of risotto and other rice dishes.

ASPARAGUS

Purchase only straight, firm asparagus stalks with compact tips; when you get them home, trim off the base ends of the stalks and wrap them in a damp dishcloth or paper towels, storing the asparagus in the refrigerator. Use within a few days of purchase.

To Peel Asparagus: To use more of each asparagus stalk, peel the skin from the lower ends of the stalk. Using a small, sharp paring knife, carefully cut beneath the thick skin at the base of the stalk; continue cutting upward in the direction of the tip, cutting more thinly as the skin becomes thinner, and ending 2–3 inches (5–7.5 cm) from the tip. Repeat on the other sides of the stalk until it is completely peeled.

BLANCH

The term *blanch* describes partially cooking an ingredient, usually a vegetable, by immersing it in a large quantity of boiling water for anywhere from a few seconds to a few minutes, depending upon the ingredient, the size of the pieces and the recipe.

BREAD CRUMBS

Among their many culinary uses, dried bread crumbs form a crunchy, golden coating on supplì. Bread crumbs are an excellent use of day-old bread.

To Make Dried Bread Crumbs: Start with a good-quality country-style loaf made of unbleached wheat flour, with a firm, coarse-textured crumb. Cut away the crusts and crumble the bread by hand, in a blender or in the work bowl of a food processor with the metal blade. Spread the crumbs on a baking sheet and dry them slowly, about 1 hour, in an oven set at its lowest temperature. Store in a tightly covered container at room temperature.

BROCCOLI

This popular green cruciferous vegetable, a relative of the cabbage, finds its way into many rice dishes, most often in the form of its small flowering buds, called florets.

To Cut Florets: Cut the flowerlike buds or clusters from the ends of the stalks, including about 1 inch (2.5 cm) of stem with each floret. Reserve the stalks for another use; they can, for example, be peeled of their tough, fibrous outer layers, then be sliced and stir-fried or steamed until tender.

GARLIC

Popular worldwide as a flavoring ingredient, this pungent bulb is best purchased in whole heads (or bulbs) composed of individual cloves, to be separated from the head as needed. Use

1. To peel, place the clove on a work surface and cover it with the side of a large knife. Press down to crush the clove slightly; slip off the dry skin.

2. To mince, use a sharp knife to cut the peeled clove into thin slices. Then cut across the slices to make thin strips.

3. Using a gentle rocking motion, cut back and forth across the strips to mince them into fine particles.

4. Alternatively, press the peeled clove through a garlic press.

within 1 to 2 weeks, as it can shrivel and lose its flavor with prolonged storage.

LEEKS

Grown in sandy soil, these leafy-topped, multi-layered vegetables require thorough cleaning.

To Clean a Leek: Trim the tough ends of the dark green leaves. Trim the roots. If a recipe calls for the white part only, trim the dark green leaves where they meet the slender pale green part of the stem. Starting about 1 inch (2.5 cm) from the root end, slit the leek lengthwise. Vigorously swish the leek in a basin or sink filled with cold water. Continue rinsing and draining until no dirt remains between the tightly packed pale green portion of the leaves.

NUTS

Many varieties of nuts may be used to add rich flavor, protein and crunchy texture to rice dishes.

To Toast Nuts: Toasting brings out the full flavor and aroma of nuts. To toast any kind of nut, preheat an oven to 325°F (165°C). Spread the nuts in a single layer on a baking sheet and toast in the oven, stirring once, until they just begin to change color, 5-10 minutes. Alternatively, toast nuts in a dry heavy frying pan over low heat, stirring frequently to prevent scorching.

To Chop Nuts: Spread the nuts in a single layer on a nonslip cutting surface. Using a chef's knife, carefully chop the nuts with a gentle rocking motion. Alternatively, put a handful or two of nuts in the work bowl of a food processor with the metal blade or a blender and use a few rapid on-off pulses to chop the nuts to the desired consistency. Be careful not to process the nuts too long, or their oils will be released and the nuts will turn into a paste.

PEAS

Freshly shelled sweet garden peas are one of the great delicacies of early summer; at other times of year, frozen peas—particularly the very small variety sometimes labeled petite peas—are an acceptable substitute. Seek out bright green, unblemished, well-filled pods that snap when bent.

To Shell Fresh Peas: Grasp the pea pod at the stem end and snap it, pulling along the pod to string it. With your thumbs, press down on the seam of the pod to pop it open, exposing the peas.

PEPPERS

Large, sweet-fleshed bell peppers (capsicums) may be used as colorful main ingredients or lively accents in a wide range of rice dishes. They are most common in the unripe green form, although ripened red, yellow, creamy pale yellow, orange and purple-black types may also be found.

To Seed Raw Peppers: Cut the pepper in half lengthwise with a sharp knife. Pull out the stem section from each half, along with the cluster of seeds attached to it. Remove any remaining seeds, along with any thin white membranes, or ribs, to which they are attached.

To Roast Peppers: Preheat a broiler (griller). Seed and derib the peppers as directed above. Place the pepper halves on a broiler pan, cut-side down, and broil (grill) until the skins blister and turn black. Transfer the peppers to a paper or heavy-duty plastic bag and let stand until the peppers soften, about 10 minutes. Using your fingertips or a small knife, peel off the blackened skins. Then tear or cut the peppers as directed in the recipe.

SHELLFISH

All shellfish should be purchased fresh and in season from a reputable merchant. They should be free of odor, giving off only a fresh clean scent of the sea. Bivalves and mollusks such as clams and mussels should be alive when purchased, closing tightly when handled before cooking; avoid any that gape open, as well as those that remain shut after cooking.

CLAMS Prized for their sweet, tender flesh, these bivalve mollusks must first be scrubbed under cold running water with a small, stiff-bristled brush, then soaked in a mixture of $1/3$ cup salt to 1 gallon of water for 1 hour. Rinse well before using. Check all the clams carefully, discarding any with shells not tightly closed. Refrigerate until use.

MUSSELS These popular, bluish black-shelled bivalves require special cleaning. Rinse the mussels thoroughly under cold running water. One at a time, hold them under the water and scrub with a firm-bristled brush to remove any stubborn dirt. Just before cooking, firmly grasp the fibrous beard attached to the side of each mussel and pull it off. Check all the mussels carefully, discarding any with shells not tightly closed. Refrigerate until use.

Shrimp (Prawns) Fresh, raw shrimp are generally sold with the heads removed but the shells still intact.

To Peel and Devein Shrimp: Using your thumbs, split open the thin shell along the inner curve, between its two rows of legs. Peel away the shell, taking care—if the recipe calls for it—to leave the last segment with the tail fin intact and attached to the meat. Using a small, sharp knife, carefully make a shallow slit along the back, just deep enough to expose the long, usually dark veinlike intestinal tract. With the tip of the knife or your fingers, lift up and pull out the vein and discard it.

SQUASHES

Hard, orange-fleshed winter squashes such as acorn and butternut squashes and pumpkin pair well with rice.

To Prepare Winter Squash: Cut the squash open with a heavy, sharp kitchen knife, using a kitchen mallet, if necessary, to tap the knife carefully once it is securely wedged in the squash. With a sharp-edged spoon, scrape out all seeds and fibers from the squash's flesh before cutting it as directed in the recipe.

TOMATOES

During summer, when tomatoes are in season, use the best red or yellow sun-ripened tomatoes you can find. At other times of year, plum tomatoes, sometimes called Roma or egg tomatoes, are likely to have the best flavor and texture. For cooking, canned whole, diced or crushed plum tomatoes

are also good. Small cherry tomatoes, barely bigger than the fruit after which they are descriptively named, also have a pronounced flavor during their peak summer season. Store fresh tomatoes of any kind in a cool, dark place; refrigeration causes them to break down quickly. Use within a few days of purchase.

To Peel and Seed a Fresh Tomato

1. Bring a saucepan of water to a boil. Using a small, sharp knife, cut out the core of the tomato. Cut a shallow X in the opposite end.

2. Submerge the tomato for about 10 seconds in the boiling water, then remove and dip in a bowl of cold water.

3. Starting at the X, peel the skin, using your fingertips and, if necessary, the knife blade. Cut the tomatoes in half crosswise.

4. To seed, hold the tomato upside down and squeeze it gently to force out the seed sacs.

ZEST

The thin, brightly colored, outermost layer of a citrus fruit's peel, the zest contains most of its aromatic essential oils, which provide lively flavor to both savory and sweet rice dishes. When zesting citrus fruit, be careful to remove only the colored peel and not the bitter white pith. Use the strips as garnish or mince or grate the zest for recipes. After removing the zest, use the fruit for juice.

TO ZEST A CITRUS FRUIT

1. Using a zester or fine shredder, draw its thin, sharp-edged holes along the surface of the fruit to remove the zest in fine shreds.

2. Alternatively, using a vegetable peeler or a paring knife, remove the zest, then cut it into thin strips.

3. For finely grated zest, use a fine hand-held grater. Vigorously rub the fruit against the sharp teeth.

BASIC RECIPES

Designed to be made ahead, stored and added to many of the dishes throughout this volume, these basic stock recipes provide fresh, salt-free alternatives to similar commercial products.

VEGETABLE STOCK

This simple stock is suitable for vegetarian risottos. Canned, bottled or frozen chicken or vegetable broth may be substituted.

3 large onions, cut into 1-inch (2.5-cm) pieces

4 large carrots, peeled and cut into 1-inch (2.5-cm) pieces

4 celery stalks with leaves, cut into 1-inch (2.5-cm) pieces

4 fresh parsley sprigs

1 bay leaf

3 qt (3 l) water

1. In a large pot over medium heat, combine all the ingredients. Bring to a boil. Reduce the heat and simmer uncovered for 1 hour.

2. Using a strainer, strain the stock into a large bowl. Store in a tightly covered container in the refrigerator for up to 3 days or in the freezer for up to 1 week.

Makes about 7 cups (56 fl oz/1.75 l)

FISH STOCK

Use this light stock as the liquid for seafood risottos. If you don't have time to make it, bottled clam juice may be substituted.

3 lb (1.5 kg) fish bones, heads and skin from non-oily fish such as cod, sole, snapper, halibut, sea bass and monkfish

2 onions, cut into 1-inch (2.5-cm) pieces

3 celery stalks with leaves, cut into 1-inch (2.5-cm) pieces

2 cups (16 fl oz/500 ml) dry white wine

7 cups (56 fl oz/1.75 l) water

1. Remove any scales from the fish skin. Remove the gills from fish heads. Rinse bones, heads and skin.
2. In a large saucepan over medium heat, combine all the ingredients. Bring to a boil, skimming the surface occasionally to remove the fat and froth.
3. Reduce the heat and simmer gently uncovered for 30 minutes.
4. Using a strainer, strain the stock into a large bowl. Store in a tightly covered container in the refrigerator for up to 3 days or in the freezer for up to 1 month.

Makes about 6 cups (48 fl oz/1.5 l)

CHICKEN STOCK

For convenience, canned, bottled or frozen chicken broth may be used in place of this simple stock. For even more flavor, brown the chicken, onions and carrots in 1 tablespoon of olive oil before adding the water.

3 lb (1.5 kg) chicken backs and necks

2 large onions, cut into 1-inch (2.5-cm) pieces

2 large carrots, peeled and cut into 1-inch (2.5-cm) pieces

2 celery stalks with leaves, cut into 1-inch (2.5-cm) pieces

3 qt (3 l) water

2 bay leaves

4 fresh parsley sprigs

1. In a large pot over medium heat, combine all the ingredients. Bring to a boil, skimming the surface occasionally to remove the fat and froth.
2. Reduce the heat, cover partially and simmer gently for 5 hours.
3. Using a strainer, strain the stock into a large bowl. Refrigerate until the fat on the surface solidifies.
4. Skim the solid fat from the surface before using. Store in a tightly covered container in the refrigerator for 3 days or in the freezer for up to 3 months.

Makes about 8 cups (64 fl oz/2 l)

INDEX